UNSTUCK TOGETHER

UNSTUCK TOGETHER

REFLECTIONS ON PARENTING, PARTNERSHIP, AND PACKING FROM 303 DAYS ON THE ROAD WITH A BABY

LAURA WEIDMAN POWERS

NEW DEGREE PRESS

UNSTUCK TOGETHER

ISBN   978-1-63676-597-6   *Paperback*

978-1-63676-242-5   *Kindle Ebook*

978-1-63676-243-2   *Ebook*

To Mike. And to "Ella."
To #2. And to our next adventure.

CONTENTS

——

INTRODUCTION   1

DAY 1: ROME   5

THE DECISION TO QUIT EVERYTHING   7

THE CALL   15

THE ADJUSTMENT   19

THE UNIVERSITY'S GIFTS   25

GRUPO DI MAMME   *29*

FRIDAY NIGHTS IN THE PIAZZA   33

HIRE A BABYSITTER WHEN YOU TRAVEL   37

HOW TO PACK FOR A YEAR   45

THE ACCIDENTAL MINIMALIST(ISH)   51

THE LUGGAGE   55

WORK LIFE BALANCE   59

WORKING WITHOUT INFRASTRUCTURE   65

YOU HAVE ONE FRIEND   69

100 DATE NIGHTS   73

TRAVELING VS VACATIONING   77

LAST MINUTE TRAVEL FOR THE NON-SPONTANEOUS   81

WHEN IN ITALY, FOLLOW YOUR STOMACH   85

BABY STEPS   89

ON TO AMSTERDAM   93

THE BELLS TOLL FOR ME   97

BABY MUSIC CLASS   101

BRING YOUR BABY TO MOROCCO   105

RUG SHOPPING IN MARRAKECH   109

GHOST TOWNS IN SPAIN   113

MAY ELLA ONE DAY CLIMB A HUMAN TOWER   119

THE REFRAME   123

IF YOU FIND YOURSELVES IN FRANCE   127

EVERYONE HAS BAD DAYS   133

250 MEALS OUT   141

THE DECISION TO RETURN   145

GOING ON VACATION   149

SETTLING IN   153

WORK IT OUT   159

RETURN TO REAL LIFE   163

WORKING WITHOUT INFRASTRUCTURE PART 2   167

WHERE IS THE BACON?   171

UNSTUCK TOGETHER   175

ACKNOWLEDGEMENTS   179

INTRODUCTION

———

In September 2017, I was stressed. I was six months pregnant, uncomfortable on a good day. I was spending all my waking hours trying to lead my company through a rapidly escalating crisis. While on the phone with lawyers and in meetings with employees, I'd work hard to project confidence, competence, and professionalism. Every time I'd hang up the phone or walk out of a room, I'd cry.

I was tired; not just physically, not just mentally, but existentially tired.

I felt trapped.

I had a promising career in Silicon Valley. I was CEO of a social impact startup I'd co-founded, a role that had landed me in the pages of newspapers and magazines, on stages across the country, and giving interviews on television and radio. We were changing lives, shifting culture, and building power in a way that felt impactful and good.

My husband Mike's career was going well, too. A few years earlier he had made the transition from the practically obligatory post-law school job as an associate at a corporate firm to a more interesting—and more humane—role at a top tech company.

We had a rent-controlled apartment in the middle of San Francisco, a sun-drenched deck filled with succulents we'd collected over the years. And after years of trying, we had finally a baby on the way.

On the surface, things were going great.

Under the surface, the water was murky. Neither of us were happy at our jobs and we were struggling to envision what better could come next. We'd fallen out of love with San Francisco as it had morphed over the decade from quirky-hippie to cookie-cutter-techie. We were far from our East Coast-based families at the very moment when we were starting our own.

We knew we needed to make a change, but we felt stuck. We didn't know how much change to make, or how to go about it.

Then, one Saturday afternoon that September, during a twenty-minute conversation I had with eight other women, it all became clear.

And that is how, one year later, in September 2018, it came to be that we changed everything.

We had quit our jobs. We had sold most of our things and given up our rent-controlled apartment. We were saying goodbye to San Francisco, our home for the last decade. Our remaining belongings were moving to New York, but we weren't—not yet. First, we were going to travel. For a year. With Ella, our eight-month-old baby girl.

In September 2019, after 303 days abroad followed by more than a month spent living in guest bedrooms, we moved to Brooklyn, New York. We got our things out of storage and marveled at what it was like to no longer live out of suitcases and to have access to more than three pairs of pants. We strove to integrate into our new Brooklyn community, joining the local food co-op and putting our daughter in a Spanish immersion, Waldorf-inspired, Montessori playschool that was just a short walk from us in Bed-Stuy. We found jobs in our respective fields and began the now-foreign ritual of commuting to an office and spending time apart from one another all day.

It was shocking how quickly our lives returned to "normal."

Until, of course, the COVID-19 pandemic hit New York in early 2020 and we found ourselves in the epicenter of an experience that was stressful and strange in a new way. We were suddenly isolated again, needing to draw on every lesson we'd learned while traveling about how to function together as a family in unfamiliar circumstances.

It's now September 2020, and we're on the eve of another set of changes. We bought a house a mile away from our Brooklyn rental, and every evening we sort through our belongings, placing items into boxes, trying to pare down to the essentials. We have another hard-won baby on the way. We are six months into this global pandemic that has upended our assumptions about what life would be like in New York upon our return—but has oddly confirmed the relevance of many learnings and takeaways from our nomadic life abroad.

There are many times when I still feel the tension between putting down roots and getting stuck. But the sense of being trapped and the feelings of angst are gone. They've been replaced with a feeling of agency. Because now I know that I'm not actually stuck. As hard as the quitting, the leaving, the traveling, and the returning was—I now know it's possible. And I'd do it all again.

As ambitious, career-, and impact-oriented as I am, I now believe that "leaning in" is overrated; sometimes leaning out or going sideways is just what the doctor ordered. Changing everything doesn't have to mean you're rejecting anything. And if you set something aside gently enough, it might just be waiting for you when you are ready for it again.

I believe that you can never know where the road not taken may lead, but you can always change the road you're on. And when you're stuck in a rut, sometimes getting out of it is its own reward.

Maybe next time the change I need to make won't involve a passport or a one-way flight. I don't know. What I do know is that, in the future, no matter how stuck I may feel, it's possible to get unstuck. And that knowledge in itself is freeing.

The essays in this book are adapted from the blog I kept while on this year of travel, exploration, and reflection. They trace our journey: from the decision to leave our San Francisco lives, to the series of experiences we had on our trip, to musings on what we learned and the choices we made upon our return. They also include some final reflections from a year after our trip ended.

My thoughts are at times unpolished. And in some cases, I suspect I won't fully unpack my experiences or extract the morals and lessons until years from now, long after these words are published. I expect to laugh at some of my naïveté or lack of insightfulness down the line.

Nonetheless, I hope there is value in my sharing my experiences and the insights I do have, at this moment. More specifically, I hope that the stories I share in this book inspire you—should you ever need it—to grab those closest to you, and to get unstuck, together, too.

Laura Weidman Powers
September 2020

DAY 1: ROME

Why is there a picture of a horse on that jar?

I stared stupidly at the shelf. I was jet-lagged. I scanned the next shelf down, looking for vegetable purees; maybe something with purple carrots or kale. Something rated "six months and up." Nothing too chunky, as Ella, my eight-month-old daughter, still didn't have many teeth.

Preferably the puree would be in pouch form, making it easier to not double dip the spoon, which, our San Francisco pediatrician's office had explained to me, could cause the bacteria in my daughter's mouth to colonize the baby food. Then, when she later ate her second serving, somehow that same bacteria that came from her own mouth would become harmful. Once I had given Ella some day-old sweet potato and the invisible mold on it had caused her to break out in hives. She did not seem to notice or mind, but I understood hives to be a sign of something bad. If not bad medically, then bad parenting.

We'd given up our spot in that exclusive pediatric practice when we left San Francisco for Rome. *Who would I call now if Ella got hives? How did one even say "hives" in Italian?*

I focused once again on the baby food display in front of

me in the little Roman grocery store. On the next shelf down the jars had pictures of bunny rabbits.

What kind of mother leaves the comfort of her ritzy-hippie San Francisco life to bring her eight-month-old baby on an international adventure with no end date? The voice in my head berated me.

My husband, Mike, and I had confidently decided to pack only enough baby food and diapers for seventy-two hours. We'll be in Rome for six weeks, after all, and they have their own babies there! And who knows where we'll go after Rome? We can't carry American supplies forever!

And now, here I was, twenty-four hours into our open-ended trip, choosing between pureed horse and bunny rabbits, no veggie blend in sight. The line between confidence and ignorance was beginning to feel thin.

I wanted to tap someone on the shoulder. Excuse me, am I missing something? In Italy, is this what babies eat? Because, if so, I don't think I'm ready for this.

That very evening at a dinner party I'd be told that, actually, most babies in Italy eat nothing of the sort. They just eat food. And Ella, who had been invited along, would underscore the point by consuming her very first antipasti.

Learning to feed an infant in Italy—with forkfuls of food off my plate instead of specially-made organic veggie blend purees—was only the first of many experiences over the course of our year of travel that would cause me to wonder if the things I'd taken for granted as normal at home were anything but. If somehow the aspirations in my life that seemed obviously right, now considered with a shift in context, were in fact unimportant.

Which was, of course, what prompted the trip in the first place.

THE DECISION TO QUIT EVERYTHING

————

In the fall of 2017, I met up with a group of eight women I'd gone to business school with for the weekend. This was not a girls' weekend.

Of course, it was a weekend of all women, but the focus was not relaxing, or the spa, or gossip, or wine, or even bonding or hanging out. I wouldn't even consider all these women to be particularly good friends.

Rather the focus of this weekend was on self-discovery, reflection, connection, and learning.

At our fifth-year business school reunion in the spring of 2015, my friend Lindsay had called a meeting. She messaged nine women from our class—close friends and women she wished she'd been closer to—and asked us to all meet her outside the alumni center. She had a proposal.

Lindsay was missing the deep, facilitated connections with women that business school had been adept at fostering through structured interaction. These sorts of moments just didn't happen organically in her day-to-day life.

"Are any of the rest of you feeling that way?" she asked. There were some murmurs of assent. She continued: "What if we self-organized a retreat, let's say once a year. Everyone commits to prioritizing it. We all pitch in to plan and facilitate it, and we try to approximate some of that connection and support on an ongoing basis?"

I knew exactly the feeling she was describing. I had myself felt unsatisfied with the way much of my social life in San Francisco seemed to revolve around happy hours rather than heart-to-hearts. Friends from the first twenty-five years of my life were mostly back on the East Coast, and I knew that creating relationships to rival those would take more than the few years I'd been living in the Bay Area. I was craving deeper connection. But I was skeptical that an annual girls' weekend with a group of acquaintances could solve for this.

But, eight of the nine were game and, not wanting to be left out, I agreed to show up that fall to a condo by the coast for a weekend away with these women, some of whom I barely knew, with the explicit purpose of getting vulnerable and pushing myself to define and reassess some of the priorities and values that were guiding my life.

That first weekend in 2015 we covered everything from personal finances to ambition to dynamics with adult siblings. The second weekend, a year later, extended these themes and touched on relationships, motherhood, entrepreneurship, and self-care. The topics were sourced by the group a few weeks before, and folks volunteered to facilitate different sessions or to arrange meals and snacks. We all pitched in, and all participated, even when it was uncomfortable or when we were being stretched.

And yet, despite how real and deep past weekends had been, I did not anticipate that the 2017 weekend would include a conversation that would set into motion some of the most dramatic changes in my life to date.

***

Fall of 2017 I was balancing the added demands of pregnancy with the ongoing demands of being a CEO. And I was in the thick of a particularly challenging stretch. That weekend I was playing defense against a senior employee who was threatening to destroy the company if we didn't give in to his demands. I was on the phone with lawyers, the board, and keeping my laptop within arm's reach. It was the third weekend in a row that I'd been taking calls at all hours, soothing the erratic executive, then creating contingency plans with lawyers as soon as we hung up. I was stressed, I was exhausted, I was not happy.

I loved my company, but I had a suspicion that my time as its leader had run its course. Besides the day-to-day challenges I was managing, the organization also needed a strategic shift, and I was beginning to come to the conclusion that I was not the right person to lead us through it. I was just too tired.

I was so tired that lately I was finding it hard to even think far enough ahead to contemplate things like strategy. My immediate priority was to neutralize some of the greatest threats to the organization—and to just get through the day. Then I could think about what was next.

I had been thinking like that for a while: *I just have to do X and then I can think about what's next.*

It seemed logical, but it was dawning on me that there was a fatal flaw in this thinking. There was not going to be a natural break for reflection. At work, projects overlapped, responsibilities persisted, and commitments to attend or speak at events were made weeks or months in advance. When I overlaid that on personal plans and concerns, I started to realize that there was simply not going to be a point when everything would stop to give me a chance to think things through uninterrupted.

Yet without that pause, I was feeling trapped on a runaway train of doing, managing, and reacting with no chance for a break for reflection. I could not figure out how to give myself the time I needed to pause and to plan. I was stuck.

Until that third retreat weekend in September 2017.

***

One of the last sessions of the weekend was led by Julia. She had taken some of the principles from the book *Design Your Life* and adapted them into a short workshop. We were all to spend a few minutes envisioning three different futures for ourselves. One of the futures that we'd present back to the group was supposed to be "wild"—a wild idea for what your life could look like in the next few years.

I don't remember my other two futures, because they quickly ceased to matter. When it was my turn to share, I described my wild future. In it, I was traveling full-time and writing about my adventures.

I knew this was crazy. I was CEO of a prominent non-profit that was poised for massive impact and also under threat. I was married to someone who had his own career and aspirations and friends, not to mention a job in an office where he was expected to show up every day. I was pregnant. There was no way I was going to magically become a nomad blogger.

There was a short pause in the room and then the reactions began. And they were unanimous.

"Actually, there is not *no* way."

"You can do this."

"If it is what you want, you can do it."

I did not believe it at first. But rather than continue the exercise and move on to the next person, the group stayed with me. They helped me think through what my company needed, was ready for, could weather. And what I needed, was ready for, and could allow myself to dream.

I had thought I needed a magical convergence of personal and professional forces to permit me to have a long period of reflection in order to get unstuck. It turns out I needed some very smart, empathetic, analytical women who could understand my competing needs and commitments and desires. And I needed their undivided attention for about twenty minutes.

Having this group coach me through the process of naming dreams I'd never before allowed myself to articulate was incredible. Having them coach me to chart a path to realizing those dreams was invaluable. There were times in the conversation when I felt completely overwhelmed just trying to process the clarity that was dawning when I could see my life through a prism of several other selfless perspectives.

The whole piece of the conversation centered on me could not have been more than about twenty minutes. But it was deeply affecting. Where before I had been myopic, unable to even find the mental space to look ahead, now I could now see possibility. That twenty minutes changed my next twenty-four months completely.

I left the weekend with a conviction: I am going to do this. When I got in my car at the end of the weekend to drive up to

San Francisco, I knew with certainty that my husband and I would both quit our jobs and we would travel for an extended period of time. And, you know what? I would blog about it.

***

On the drive home I called Mike on the phone: "We're going to travel. We're going to quit, and we're going to travel."

Mike had been confused when he picked up the phone. We generally only called each other for urgent needs, otherwise a text would suffice. And since I was pregnant there was always the possibility that a phone call was not just urgent but an emergency. So it took him a moment to process this revelation that felt so urgent to me that it could not wait the forty-five minutes it would take me to drive home.

"We... what?"

I repeated myself. He considered what I was saying. I imagined him thinking back to the conversations we'd had about how we always wanted to travel more, how we someday wanted to leave the Bay Area, how he was frustrated by parts of his job. I imagined him recalling his intention to focus on family and his disgust with living under the current presidential administration. All the expressions of discontent that, on their own perhaps weren't much, but collectively added up to a life that made sense on paper yet wasn't fulfilling in practice.

And now, he'd picked up the phone, perhaps feeling light trepidation that something was wrong, and without so much as a greeting, I had just announced that we were going to upend everything.

Secretly I hoped that by conveying the information as a declaration rather than posing it as a question, I would somehow retain the conviction I had felt surrounded by the warm, wise women I had just left behind. Already I had the sense that if I didn't keep speaking this intention out loud— and if I couldn't get Mike to share it—it would fade and risk becoming not a plan, but a regret.

Mike was silent for a moment. I knew it was dawning on him that the biggest thing holding us back from doing something like this was not in fact him—it was me. And specifically, it was my sense of responsibility to my company.

"You're going to leave your company?" he asked.

It was a question, not an accusation, but part of me started silently screaming at myself: *You can't do that! How can you do that?!* My inner voice was deafening. If I hadn't been driving, I would have covered my ears.

But another part of me had my newfound wisdom from the weekend: *Hush. You can do it, and you will do it. Not everyone will be happy with your choice, but it is what you want, and there is a path. We will help you find it and walk it.*

I am blessed with, or perhaps stuck with, a mentality that for every problem, there is a solution. It may not be obvious or easy, but it's out there and with enough diligence and digging, shifting and strategizing, it can be uncovered. It's a sort of optimism-by-effort philosophy. Prior to that weekend, I had been completely focused on solving the problem: *How can I best run my company?* And now my focus completely shifted. Now I was solving the problem: *How can I not run a company at all?*

To be honest, it still seemed a nearly insurmountable goal. Nothing had changed in terms of the company or my role from before the weekend to after it. The threats and the responsibilities were the same. But I'd gained perspective— eight perspectives—and I now felt confident that there was a solution out there.

"I am going to leave my company," I said. "And then we can go."

"Alright then!" Mike responded. I could hear the energy in his voice. "I can't wait."

THE CALL

The process of disentangling myself from my company is a
story for another time. It was fraught and it was complicated,
but, as those eight women had promised, it was possible.

It was in the midst of this process, soon after I gave birth
to my daughter, that my friend Kyla reached out. She had
been consulting for a university in Rome, which was setting up an honors program in social entrepreneurship. They
were looking for their first social entrepreneur in residence
to teach two seminars and give a public lecture on campus.

"I know you're on maternity leave, and I don't even know
if you're thinking about work stuff right now," she started.
"But I know you're co-teaching a course this spring, and they
like that you'll have that experience. And you've got the social
entrepreneur piece, and the Silicon Valley thing gives you a
perspective that will be fascinating to the students in Rome.
I need to get final approval, but I want to pitch you—I think
it's a perfect fit."

The problem was, she went on, she knew I was a CEO, my
life was based in San Francisco, and I had a newborn. This

opportunity would entail spending three weeks in Rome in the fall. It was a longshot, but… was I interested?

I couldn't believe it. My transition was going to be announced publicly in a few weeks. Here I was, six months after that girls' weekend, and I had almost managed the hard part: stepping down as CEO and disentangling myself from the company that had been so central to my life for the last six years. And now the next piece of the puzzle that had been flummoxing us as of late—a start date and first destination for our trip, a way to make the plan concrete—was practically falling into my lap. It was exactly what we needed to ensure we'd turn this idea from fantasy into reality: a deadline. Show up in Rome, Italy by October 1.

I imagined Kyla on the other end of the line, waiting out the awkwardly long pause while I processed the fact that she had brought me exactly what I needed without knowing it.

"Do it," I said. "Pitch me. I'm interested. I'll be there. We'll be there!"

"Great," Kyla said, oblivious to how momentous this phone conversation was. "Stay tuned!"

A few weeks later she texted with the good news: *They love you! Book flights! See you in Rome!*

I opened a web browser and contemplated the thousands of airline miles I'd racked up over the years traveling for my company. They represented countless meetings, conferences, and speaking engagements. They brought to mind endless sets of talking points that were second nature; all of which I'd never use again. I had formally, publicly stepped down as CEO a few weeks earlier, and my last day at the company was scheduled for later in the month.

The airline miles were an artifact of an era that was coming to a close. In a few clicks I converted a good portion of them into three one-way tickets from San Francisco to Rome, leaving the country on September 30 and arriving just in time on October 1.

I closed the web browser and stared at the blank screen. I'd never booked one-way tickets before. The flights were still months away, but simply booking them was a milestone. In that moment, I'd taken an important step. This idea to quit our jobs, sell our things, pack up our baby and go—it was no longer an idea. It was now a plan.

THE ADJUSTMENT

——

On the day of our arrival in Rome, I stepped out of the glaring fluorescence of the airport terminal and into the warm night, taking a deep breath and letting my eyes adjust. I was disoriented. Just over twelve hours ago, we'd boarded the plane in San Francisco. And now, after a classic red-eye cocktail of fitful sleep, stale air, and artificial light—with an added dash of trying to remain *perfectly still* for hours on end so as not to wake Ella, asleep while balanced on my lap—we were in Rome.

I may have been exhausted but Ella, having slept for much of the flight, was now wide awake at 8:00 p.m. local time, nestled against my chest in the baby carrier, peering out at her unfamiliar surroundings. I was dragging one giant suitcase and pushing the travel stroller laden with our carry-on bags. Mike was just ahead of me. He had the second suitcase, the car seat, and the travel crib.

I was relieved to be off the plane and reunited with our luggage. I gripped the handle of my suitcase. This was all that we'd have of home for the next year. The rest of our belongings, the things we hadn't sold or donated, were on a moving truck headed west to east across the United States, destined for my parents' basement.

My relief at getting off the plane and being reunited with our luggage, my excitement at the true start of our trip, was cut with apprehension. We had made the decision—to quit our jobs, sell our things, pack up our baby, and travel—the previous fall. It was just an idea. We didn't even have a baby yet. Now, a year later, here we were, the three of us, in Rome.

I was excited, but I was nervous. There was one persistent worry in the back of my mind.

What if this trip is too hard and we have to go back? Which would immediately be followed by a sinking feeling. *Wait— there is no "back."*

We'd given up our apartment of six years and left the place we'd called home for a decade. Even if the trip didn't work out, there was no retreat to home. There was only forging ahead and finding a new home. And in the meantime, until we did that, "home" would become a transient concept for us.

***

Home that first night, and for the six weeks to follow, was student housing in the Trastevere neighborhood in Rome. Trastevere was an ancient cobblestoned collection of tiny shops, half-hidden restaurants, and churches on piazzas. Our apartment building was on a paved road at the edge of the historic area, where modernity began to creep in. Though we were a two-minute walk from Porta Portese, a gateway to the old town built in 1644, the quickest route from there to our front door was either to cut through an alley filled with giant light-up rubber duckies courtesy of the local ultra-modern hotel, or to cut through the over-illuminated lobby of a giant chain grocery store.

The contrasts continued inside our apartment. In an old building with a rickety elevator and high ceilings, each room had large doors leading onto unfurnished balconies overlooking Rome. From one room our view was of a poured concrete housing block, from another Aventine Hill topped by Parco Savello, better known as *Giardino degli Aranci* after the orange trees that rimmed its walkways. Regardless of the view, the balcony doors let in all the dirt and dust that blew by, creating a layer of grit on our floors that never seemed to go away and would stain the knees of Ella's pants as she crawled from room to room. We'd sweep twice a day for the next month until it was cool enough to keep the doors closed.

To better suit the intended student occupants, our living room had been partitioned to make an extra bedroom we didn't need, barely leaving space for a tiny couch and a small dining table. Each of our three bedrooms had two twin-sized beds. The art on the walls, inexplicably, was New York-themed, giant canvas prints of high rises in black and white with pops of color in the form of yellow taxis streaking across the images.

Mike and I had been to Rome before, but only as tourists for a few days of bopping around the major sights: Colosseum, Vatican, Trevi Fountain. This time our list of places to visit was based on a different set of priorities: the hardware store for a stovetop espresso maker, the Sunday flea market for dish towels. The *salumeria* down the block for *salumi* and a jug of olive oil. The *farmacia* for face wash, shampoo, and conditioner. The grocery store for baby food.

And so, as we got over our jetlag and filled our flat with the essentials, our days began to take shape. We'd spend some days together, grabbing an espresso and going to the playground, or putting Ella in the carrier and walking the neighborhood, visiting churches and picking up *pizza a taglio* for lunch at home while she slept. Other days we'd split up, one of us taking Ella and the other venturing farther afield to churches or museums unencumbered by a baby and the accoutrement she required and time limits she imposed.

We quickly realized that the pacing of this trip would be unlike that of any trip we'd taken before. For starters, Ella's tolerance for tourism was low. She didn't much care where she was, as long as she could be noisy and crawl on the floor. This was impossible at most tourist attractions and restaurants—really anywhere outside the house but playgrounds and piazzas. To satisfy our own wanderlust and curiosity, we'd strap her to one of our chests in the baby carrier as we explored Rome, but we'd always have to balance that time with downtime at home where she could be free to explore her world on her own terms.

On top of that, we were spending weeks in Rome, not days, as we would on a typical vacation. And the longer we spent there, the more we realized how we were only scratching the city's surface. Prior to this trip, I used to think I'd "done" a place if I'd spent a few days there seeing major sites and eating the must-try foods. The more time we spent in Rome, the more laughable this concept seemed. In six weeks we didn't make it through half of our to-do list, and I realized I'd never be "done" with Rome.

This helped set the tone for the rest of the trip. No matter how short or long we spent in a place for the rest of the year, we released ourselves of any pressure to hit all the major attractions. We'd each pick a thing or two that we genuinely wanted to do, and wouldn't bother with the rest, no matter how lauded in the travel books. The truth is, being packed into an experience with hundreds of tourists, navigating crowds day in and day out—it simply wasn't tolerable to do that for a year on end.

So in Rome, and in most places thereafter, we spent many days in residential neighborhoods, visiting small shops and cafes and playgrounds and contenting ourselves with the notion that it was more interesting to do that in Oslo and Asilah and Amsterdam than it would be to do it yet again in our old neighborhood in San Francisco.

THE UNIVERSITY'S GIFTS

—

After landing in Italy, we had only a few days to get settled before I began teaching. Since our typical travel benchmark was a vacation, it felt strange to me to start our trip by working. But it was an apt reminder that this was to be a year of exploration and adventure, not leisure and vacation. And, I quickly realized, the role at the university ended up being a gift.

The university sat at the top of *Gianicolo* hill overlooking our slice of Trastevere. It had originally been a monastery. The classrooms and administrative buildings were behind stone walls, the entrance through a tall iron gate. The gravel courtyard was dotted with iron chairs, usually filled with students doing their homework or collaborating on group projects. There was a vending machine in the student lounge that, for a euro coin, dispensed espresso in tiny plastic cups. My office was up a narrow staircase in the back of the main building.

I shared this office with a woman named Iman, who was organizing the social entrepreneurship programming and the initiative at the university that had brought me to Rome. Iman was the first gift of the university—she would end up being more than a colleague; she and her husband Lorenzo would become our tour guides, babysitters, dinner partners, and friends. They transformed our time in Rome, setting the tone for the rest of our trip, reminding us how much we valued the experience of *living* in a place rather than *visiting* it and setting a standard that we would chase for the rest of our travels.

The second gift was a reminder that I enjoyed teaching. Even in the rushed format of a two-week seminar, and even with an untested curriculum that I'd developed in between packing boxes in San Francisco. I filed the feeling of satisfaction I experienced in the classroom away in the back of my head. After finding that being CEO of a startup was as painful as it was rewarding, it was a relief to do something that felt meaningful and challenging but devoid of angst.

The third gift was perhaps the most unexpected, but the most enduring. It was the gift of a reframing of our vision of parenting Ella as a baby—at least in as much as it concerned her eating habits.

***

Our first week in Rome I attended a formal event hosted by the university, featuring a speaker followed by a sit-down dinner in an old hotel. Iman was there, as was Kyla, my friend who had pitched me for the posting. We sipped champagne on the terrace, mingling, and they were introducing me to my new colleagues.

"Ah! We are happy to meet you!" professors and administrators and deans said. "But we heard you'd have a baby with you, where is she?"

When I explained that my husband was home with the baby, they seemed dismayed. "Why didn't you bring them both?"

The thought had never crossed my mind. This was a formal evening. There had been a lecture. My colleagues were in suits. I had heard Italy was baby-friendly, but this seemed a bit extreme.

"Well," the dean of the university sighed, finally. "You didn't bring them tonight, okay. But bring them to our dinner tomorrow."

So the following night, Mike, Ella and I took the bus together from our flat in Trastevere into the upscale residential Gianicolense neighborhood at the top of a hill overlooking Rome. We followed the directions I'd been given down a narrow side street to a little family-run Sardinian restaurant where we'd join the dean, the university president, Kyla, and a few others for an intimate dinner party.

I was self-conscious about bringing an infant to a work dinner. In San Francisco we had brought Ella out to several restaurants, but we always timed our meals and happy hours so that she was sleeping. Tonight, this jet-lagged baby was wide awake for our 8:00 p.m. dinner.

I texted Kyla: *Are you SURE this will be ok??*

But the moment we crossed the threshold my apprehension turned to surprise.

"*Ciao! Ciao, piccola!*" The owner of the restaurant rushed over to meet us at the door and to squeeze Ella's feet.

She was delighted. Before we could even sit down, she was discussing what she would make for Ella. "*E per la bambina? Penne all'amatriciana? Spaghetti alla nonna?*"

I was momentarily stunned. The woman was asking my daughter which pasta dish she would like. *Couldn't she see that she was just a baby?* I couldn't tell if I was more shocked that the assumption was that she would eat pasta, or that she needed her own order of it.

"Oh, *sta bene*, she's fine, *grazie*, no thank you!" I stammered. The proprietor and I went back and forth a few more times—she was very insistent on the *amatriciana*—before I finally said "Okay, *va bene*, we'll share!"

I thought back to my afternoon trip to the grocery store the day after our arrival and recalled the lack of appealing baby purees, a level of awareness dawning on me.

We got settled at the table, and the dean leaned over to me, passing a plate. "Has she had anchovies? These are delicious!"

Ella had tried solid food in San Francisco before we left, but it had been foods carefully selected off a pre-approved list from her pediatrician, fed to her at home under close supervision in case of allergic reaction. I had understood that, as a baby, she needed to be fed with great intentionality and great care. It had never occurred to me that her eating habits could simply mirror mine, or those of others around the table at a dinner party.

"*Ecco, bambina!*" the dean urged, gesturing to the anchovies as she smiled at Ella.

Ella leaned over and picked up one of the tiny fish with her fist, then shoved the head in her mouth, delighted.

I guess we wouldn't be needing jarred food after all.

GRUPO DI MAMME

———

A week or so into our time at Rome, my colleague at the university, Iman, mentioned that there was a daycare in her building that seemed to have some playgroups in the mornings. Mike, Ella and I headed out for a walk one morning and decided to drop by to check it out. The woman at the front desk was gracious but spoke only Italian. My Italian was beginner at best, so after some back-and-forth she suggested that I simply drop into the playgroup in progress at the moment. I scooped Ella out of the stroller, we took off our shoes, and the receptionist pulled open a sliding wood door and ushered us through. As I turned to look back at Mike, she quickly pushed the door shut.

I found myself standing over a circle of women sitting in dim lighting with an assortment of infants crawling around, breastfeeding, or napping on their backs. The group leader looked up and beckoned me to join. Two women made some space, and I awkwardly crossed the room to take a seat with Ella on the floor.

One of the women was speaking in rapid Italian; she was animated, maybe a bit sad, and I struggled to follow.

Someone passed me a handout that I placed behind me while I got Ella settled. Once she was content on her back with one of the toys I'd grabbed from the corner, I picked the handout up again.

The first thing that caught my attention was the imagery on it which seemed to be vaguely… pornographic. I looked at the title: *Il Rapporti Sessuale Dopo Il Parto*. It took me a moment to translate it in my head: Sexual Intercourse after Childbirth.

I blinked, my situation dawning on me. I looked up and tuned into what this woman was sharing. She was talking about the last time she and her husband tried to have sex and how difficult it was since the baby—she was always crying at the most inopportune times!

I then realized why the room was so dim. Over her head there was a projector humming, and on the opposite wall, behind where I was seated, was an image of a giant vagina. *Was this what a playgroup was like in Italy?* When it was my turn to introduce myself, I shared in my broken Italian my name and the fact that I was here in Rome for a month, and then quickly thanked everyone for welcoming me and turned to my neighbor before I could be asked any questions about my own postpartum sex life.

When the hour was over, the group leader introduced herself to me and asked if I'd like to come back. "Or there's an English language group on Fridays."

"Ah, yeah, um, no, this was great, but, like, my Italian… English sounds great, thanks, see you then!"

I rushed out to reunite with Mike. I figured I'd try the English group next and at least if I was forced to discuss my sex life it would be in a language in which I was fluent.

But, no, of course, as I discovered the following week, the English language version was nothing like the Italian moms' safe space. It was a handful of us from around the world, talking about whether we were working at the moment, which playgrounds were adjacent to excellent gelato, and which other playgroups around Rome were worth the money.

The content was more immediately useful, but I couldn't help but compare it to those Italian *mamme* sitting in the dark, talking about what really mattered to them at the moment: intimacy, not commerce.

FRIDAY NIGHTS
IN THE PIAZZA

———

After a few days of getting settled in Rome, we took our new friend Iman up on her offer to babysit Ella so Mike and I could have an evening to ourselves. The thought of leaving my child alone with a near-stranger in a foreign country did make me a little uncomfortable, but when I interrogated my feelings, I knew that it was more nerves than real risk.

After all, Iman was a friend of Kyla's, she was a colleague at the university, and, I told myself—*let's be real*—in the case that there *was* some type of emergency with Ella in Rome, she was much better off with someone who had lived there for years, spoke fluent Italian, and had extended family in the city, than she was with me, who barely knew the street names and had only memorized the Italian words for the most common illnesses (luckily *vomito* and *diarrea* are both cognates).

So, one evening Mike and I put Ella in the stroller and dropped her off with Iman and her husband Lorenzo at their apartment, then went for an *aperitivo* nearby. When it was time to pick Ella up to bring her home for bedtime, I texted Iman. No answer.

We walked back over to their apartment and rang the bell. No answer.

Okay, I thought. *No problem.* I texted Iman again. No answer.

Mike and I stared at each other nervously. We knew it was probably *just fine*. But also... *Where were they? Where was the nearest hospital again?*

"Let's check the piazza," Mike said. The neighborhood piazza was a few blocks away, and Iman had described to us earlier how it was *the* multi-generational hangout spot on Friday nights, with everyone arranged by age on different corners of the square. Teenagers on one side, *nonni e nonne* on another, and parents keeping an eye on younger kids running around the center. *Perhaps they were there?*

As we approached the piazza, we scanned the scene, looking for Ella, Iman, and Lorenzo. No sign of them. Then we noticed a small crowd on one side, a group of five or six girls fussing over something.

No, someone. Ella was standing up in her stroller, smiling gleefully as these eight-year-old girls exclaimed over her. *"Che bella! Piccola bambina!"*

As we drew closer Iman saw us and shouted a greeting. The girls all turned as well. *"Ah! Ecco la mama! Ecco la papa! Gli Americani!"* They were overjoyed to meet the people to whom this baby belonged.

I thought back to a babysitter we had used in San Francisco. I appreciated that I could always get ahold of her via text instantaneously. But then one day as I was heading back to the apartment, I pulled up the camera feed in Ella's room to see if she would be sleeping when I got there. I was walking up the block, and when the feed loaded on my phone, I stopped short. The babysitter was cross-legged on the floor next to Ella, who was crying on her play mat. But the babysitter was not comforting her. In fact, she was not even looking at her. She was reading a book.

I remembered the anger that flooded me in that moment, to accidentally catch someone I trusted violating that trust. I switched from the monitor app on my phone to my messaging app and texted her: *On my way back!* Then I quickly switched back to the video feed. The babysitter glanced over at her buzzing phone and wrote back: *Great!* And then resumed her chapter as Ella continued to scream.

In contrast, Iman's phone was in her bag, and she and a half dozen others were giving Ella all their doting, undivided attention. Yes, she hadn't answered my ping, but we figured out where to look for her, and I didn't doubt for a minute that if there had been trouble, she would have called.

I felt the buzz of the last glass of Chianti I'd sipped at the bar warming me up pleasantly as we joined the circle welcoming us in the piazza and sat down to chat with our new friends.

HIRE A BABYSITTER
WHEN YOU TRAVEL

———

Even when we didn't have such a clear choice for a babysitter, Mike and I were committed to having childcare when we could while we traveled.

As we readied ourselves for our year abroad, Mike and I were eleven years into our relationship, and seven years into our marriage. We'd celebrated countless ups and weathered countless downs over the years together. We'd supported each other through stressful situations and learned how to collaborate on decisions. We'd clawed our way back from painful lows in our relationship via rounds of communication, commitment, and consistency.

And we'd recently navigated the transition to parenthood. While we had spent more than a decade together, we'd only had a few months' worth of adjustment to sharing that life with Ella. So while the foundation of our relationship felt strong, the foundation of our family was brand new.

Ella's arrival had of course brought on all sorts of changes for us. For one, from late 2007 when Mike and I met until early 2018 when Ella was born, I couldn't think of a time when we'd spent twenty-four hours a day together for more than about a ten-day stretch. Like many couples, we lived lives that were intersecting, but also largely parallel, spending most of our waking hours apart, at work, seeing family and friends. This felt normal.

Ella's arrival changed that. We synced up our first six weeks of parental leave and spent that stretch acclimating to our new life as a family of three. But then we'd reverted to something approximating a new normal, with professional responsibilities returning and childcare to pick up the slack.

Now, headed into this year of travel, we realized that we'd be spending nearly all of our time together as a trio, and that it would be easy for family time to eclipse everything else in our lives. We'd already largely given up our working lives, outside of my brief stretch of teaching and a day or so per week of consulting I'd committed to. That shift was deliberate.

But it also seemed possible that this construction of our lives as both parents and perma-travelers would mean much less personal time for each of us. And how on earth were we supposed to find time together as a couple?

So before we left the US, Mike and I made an intimacy-related commitment: we would hire babysitters while we traveled. We had talked to too many couples who had made it years into their child's life before they had a night out alone, and we knew that couldn't be us or we'd go nuts. Yet that's arguably what we were setting ourselves up for by constantly putting ourselves in unfamiliar environments where we knew few people and had fewer trusted relationships.

We'd hired babysitters in the evenings a few times in San Francisco. It had felt nerve-wracking enough to leave our baby with a quasi-stranger on our home turf with no language barrier. The prospect of hiring babysitters in cities and towns we were just passing through, without any personal contacts, terrified me.

On the other hand, I knew this fear was largely irrational. Caring for Ella for only a few hours at a time was relatively simple. It mostly involved playing with her, feeding her at the appointed hour, and knowing how to change a diaper. We needed someone who knew what to do in an emergency, of course, but the truth is nearly anyone we hired to come babysit would be better equipped to deal with an emergency in their hometown than we were as visitors passing through.

I'd give myself this pep talk countless times over the year, because ensuring that we had time together as a couple was, I knew, for us, non-negotiable.

The intention was there, but it still took work to make it a reality. We knew that if we were to keep up this pattern of hiring babysitters while we traveled, we'd need to be incredibly proactive about doing so.

And so, every time we picked a new destination, the first step—sometimes even before determining how we'd get there and where we'd stay—was to try to track down a babysitter. We asked friends, who asked friends of friends. We posted on social media. We asked Airbnb hosts. When all else failed, we found local websites and services that offered vetting and review systems.

Over the course of the year, Ella was watched by seventeen different babysitters in eleven countries.

***

Some were fabulous. When we were in Valencia, Spain for a month, we invested in finding a babysitter who could come a few times a week. Natalya was a mother herself, with a teenager at home, who missed being around babies. She worked hard for Ella's affection from the moment they met, bringing toys to entertain her and making up little games to play together.

One evening when Mike and I were getting ready to go out, Natalya was in the living room playing with Ella, who was fourteen months old at the time, and I walked by. They had made a set of bright interlocking plastic rings into an imaginary swimming pool, and a rubber froggy toy was going for a dip. I remember feeling shocked.

Oh! This is how you're supposed to play with a child this age!

I hadn't realized that Ella was capable of this sort of entry-level imaginary play. We spent most of our unstructured play time with her stacking things and knocking them over, rereading the same three books we'd been carrying around for weeks, or rolling a ball down the hall.

In that moment, I felt a bit guilty—but also a bit relieved. Perhaps having a babysitter come wasn't simply an investment in our marriage. It was for my own mental health, and for the health of Mike's and my relationship, yes. But with an experienced sitter, it was also rounding out Ella's development in ways that, as first-time parents detached from our community and support system, we may have been falling short.

Some babysitters took care of us as a family. We spent two months with Hind in Marrakech. We were shocked when the woman we were renting our *riad* from explained how little it would cost to have a full-time housekeeper, and that she could find someone with childcare experience. We eagerly took her up on her offer. Hind was incredible, not only helping us navigate a variety of needs in Marrakech during our stay there, keeping us organized and fed, but also became a favorite of Ella's.

And others simply brought new approaches and ways of having fun. A friend's cousin babysat Ella in the evenings in Marrakech, bringing her balloons and singing her songs in French and Arabic. In Biarritz, France, Ella's babysitter surprised us by finding a way to comb through her curly hair without tears.

Of course there were moments when Ella desperately wanted us to stay with her while we were headed out the door to something nonessential, like cocktails and dinner, and I felt some guilt over our choice to hire help.

But only one babysitter the entire year was terrible.

***

Our friends recommended a babysitter they'd used years ago in Edinburgh named Margaret. We'd booked Margaret for several nights—we were coming off three weeks where we hadn't been able to find a sitter in the rural north of Scotland and we needed some adult time.

The first night we left Ella with Margaret she seemed nice enough, though a bit dismayed that Ella was awake. "Usually they hire me after the baby's already asleep," she said in her pleasant Scottish accent.

"Mmmhmm," I replied, with an eyebrow raised, showing her around.

"And are you alright if I make some tea and watch the telly?" she asked as we kissed Ella goodbye.

"Sure," we said.

Ella started crying as we left. "That's normal!" we shouted from the hall. We believed in the quick exit philosophy.

"She'll calm down in a few minutes. Text if you need anything, we'll be nearby at dinner."

Mike and I headed out to a local restaurant, a well-reviewed Mexican place. We were thrilled by the prospect of eating one of our favorite cuisines, even if authentic Mexican food in Edinburgh seemed unlikely. We got there and put our name on the list for a table, then crossed the street to a cocktail bar. Just as I took the first sip of my drink, my phone buzzed. It was Margaret.

Don't think this is going to work!

I stared at the text, dumbfounded. We'd only been gone about thirty minutes. What did she mean?

She continued: *Not very happy!*

Did she mean Ella? Or her?

She's stopped screaming but she's still sobbing. Sorry!

Sorry? Mike and I gulped our drinks and removed our name from the Mexican restaurant's waitlist, then walked home, dejected. Ella was calm when we arrived, doing those post-meltdown shudder-breaths. They were watching the telly. Margaret looked rattled. She gathered her things and headed for the door.

"Don't like to see them unhappy, you know! Alright, then. Let me know if you'd still like me to come back on Thursday."

"I'll text you," was all I could manage.

Mike took Ella to bed, while I ordered takeout on a local delivery app. When he came out of her room, I was close to tears. We couldn't have Margaret back. We'd have to cancel all our plans all week.

"I dunno," Mike said slowly. "What if we just have her come after Ella is asleep? We'd have to move our plans a little later, but at least we'd get to go out."

I was furious at Margaret. I wanted to punish her for ruining our night out. I didn't want to hire her again and pay her to sit and watch television and drink tea. In my mind, one of the joys of getting a babysitter was the chance to skip out on the bedtime routine every now and again. And part of what I was paying for was the opportunity for Ella to get acclimated to spending time with someone else during a stretch when we were spending so much time together.

But I knew Mike was right. We had little chance of finding a replacement babysitter on such short notice—we'd already worked our connections to find Margaret. Punishing her would only punish us.

"I'll sleep on it," I said, not willing to give in so quickly. The next morning, I called our friend who'd connected us to Margaret and told her what happened.

"What?!" she said, incredulous. "I remember Margaret being great! Hang on." She hollered to her husband in the other room and told him what happened.

"We only ever hired her while the twins were asleep!" I heard him holler back.

"Welp, I didn't remember that," she said.

I sighed. Then we changed our plans so that we'd be able to leave the house after Ella was asleep. I texted Margaret. *We'll see you on Thursday.*

HOW TO PACK
FOR A YEAR

———

A few weeks before we were scheduled to leave on our trip, Mike and I began to pack. We started with a spreadsheet listing out the things we'd bring: the specific clothes, shoes, and outerwear that would be selected to sustain us for the better part of a year.

In all our past trips, we'd traveled with a carry-on suitcase each, plus a backpack or tote for things we'd need on the airplane. I had a rule that made this possible for any trip I'd ever taken before, regardless of length: Never pack for more than a week. If you're traveling for longer than that, you'll need to figure out laundry.

Our friends Stephanie and Rob, who had done an around-the-world trip the year before, had managed with two backpacks that could be cinched down to carry-on size. The few times they needed bulky items, like winter coats in Japan, they'd bought cheap versions upon arrival, and discarded them upon departure.

It was a nice idea, and the things on the first two tabs on our spreadsheet, where Mike and I listed our items, seemed like they could almost fit into two carry-ons. But then there was the third tab on our packing spreadsheet: everything Ella needed. Yes, her clothes were tiny, but her car seat, travel crib, and travel stroller were not. Not to mention bottles, books, a bare minimum of toys, and other essentials. We would not be carrying on.

We purchased two twenty-eight-inch rolling suitcases and proceeded to do a trial run of our packing. What had seemed reasonable on a spreadsheet was laughable in a suitcase. We unpacked, removed items, deleted from the spreadsheet, and tried again. On our third try we were satisfied. The suitcases were full, but not stuffed, and could be lifted—by Mike, at least.

The suitcases, however, were just the beginning. There was nothing to be done about our ancillary baby items. We needed the travel stroller for days of sightseeing. With the amount of moving around we were doing, we felt we had to bring our own car seat. Not bringing a car seat would mean renting one every time we rented a car, which would be expensive. And while in most countries, kids could ride without a car seat in taxis, we didn't feel comfortable doing that for long trips on highways to and from airports, yet with all our luggage, condemning ourselves to public transit seemed short-sighted.

We also decided to bring a travel crib. Without one, we'd be forced to either limit our lodging to places that could supply a crib, or to co-sleep with Ella. We were wary of this, and as it turned out, the one time we ended up in a situation where we had to co-sleep, Mike and I spent the whole night getting kicked in the head as Ella proved shockingly acrobatic while she slept. Lugging the travel crib was worth it.

And so, we ended up with what felt like the minimum viable collection of items for our trip. While we didn't regret the stroller, crib, or car seat, with most of the smaller things, we could have gotten by bringing less.

But at that moment, we were prone to overpacking.

***

That's because, a few months before we left, before we began the mechanics of packing, we were already mentally preparing. Never having traveled with a baby before, we decided to take a trial run locally. What did we need to bring to ensure our trip was a success? For our first trip as a family of three, we drove up to a small town in wine country just north of San Francisco. Ella was eight weeks old.

We rented a room at a roadside hotel for a night, dropped by the local winery tasting room, and made it through most of a pizza dinner by choosing seats at the bar where I could stand and bounce Ella in her carrier if she got fussy. So far, the weekend was going well. Next stop, Italy. "We can do this!" We were practically high-fiving one another.

Things began to unravel quickly after dinner. As we got ready for bed, I settled in to breastfeed Ella just before she went to sleep. At this point, Ella engaged in something I'd never heard of but would shortly be internet-searching in horror: she went on her first ever "nipple strike." This was just as it sounds. A complete refusal to breastfeed. The very nipple she had eagerly sought since birth now sent her into screaming hysterics.

For this twenty-four-hour trip where the two of us would be together the entire time, we had not thought to bring the breast pump or any bottles. And so, it was nipple or nothing. Ella chose nothing.

As Ella became hungrier, she became crankier. As she became crankier, she became louder. As she became louder, I began to panic. *The walls of this old hotel couldn't be very thick. Did we mention when we made the reservation that we had a baby? Are they going to come tell us to please keep it down? Are they aware that I would do anything to "keep it down" but that I cannot control this tiny human?*

I had read somewhere that babies can actually drink from cups long before we usually give them the chance to. I poked at my over-full breasts beginning to leak through my bra and scanned the hotel room desperately before my gaze landed on the cheap coffee maker and two ceramic mugs that came with it.

Mike was soothing Ella to no effect. "I'll be back!" I said, eyes wild, as I grabbed a mug and retreated into the tiny bathroom to do what the lactation consultant at the hospital had described as "hand expression."

I was milking myself.

I hunched over the sink and filled the cup with an inch of breastmilk, relieving my weeping boobs, and emerged from the bathroom.

"Here!" I cried triumphantly. We sat on the bed, huddled over our screaming baby, and tried to get Ella to drink breastmilk from a mug.

As would probably come as no surprise to anyone who has interacted with an eight-week-old baby, we failed.

We made it through that night by grabbing Ella any time she stirred and sticking her on my boob before she remembered she was striking and started wailing. Then Mike would rock her back to sleep while I stuck a pillow over my head, and we'd wait for the cycle to start again ninety minutes later. Exhausted and deflated, we checked out of the hotel at 7:00 a.m. and headed back to San Francisco, where Mike prepared a bottle and I made a beeline for the breast pump, vowing never to let it leave my side again.

To me, the moral of the story was clear: Pack for every eventuality, or your trip could be ruined.

***

By the time we were packing for Rome, Ella was only breastfeeding a couple times a day, and drinking confidently from a sippy cup, so the breast pump was no longer part of our lives. But the lesson I took from that first trip stuck with me: The key to a successful trip is anticipating your needs and packing perfectly. Hence the spreadsheets and the oversized suitcases.

It would take me awhile to realize that this idea of packing perfectly was an illusion; that I'd drawn the wrong lesson from our inaugural trip. On the few occasions where things did go completely sideways on our travels, there was no one thing we could have had in our suitcases that would have made our experience easier.

Instead, we would find ourselves attempting to carry fewer and fewer things as the trip went on, ruthlessly giving things away as they got worn out or outgrown. We had packed the equivalent of a medicine cabinet when we left San Francisco, and ultimately would carry only the things that we might need in the middle of the night (a thermometer, baby acetaminophen) or that we found were nearly impossible to get outside of the US (decongestant with pseudoephedrine in it).

What we learned in the end was: Pack only what you need, because you will have to carry it all, always, and while also carrying a baby. Things will go wrong, inevitably. Nothing you have in your suitcase will change that fact. Enjoy the good. Make peace with the bad. Or at least laugh at it later.

But those are lessons that I'd have to learn several times over throughout the course of the year.

THE ACCIDENTAL MINIMALIST(ISH)

Over the course of the twelve months we traveled, as we strove to carry the minimum amount possible, we'd swap out much of the contents of our suitcases. Clothes would stretch or stain, seasons would change, and Ella would grow out of everything she started with. Each time we'd leave behind a small pile of clothes in our hotel room or rental with a note: take it or toss it.

When we were preparing for the trip, I struggled with how few things I'd have space to bring: three pairs of pants, three sweaters, one jacket, one outfit for exercise.

I had always liked the ideal of minimalism. The idea that you knew, and had, exactly what you needed, and nothing more. Yet I'd long believed that, admiration for the concept aside, I was incompatible with the minimalist lifestyle.

For one, I imagined minimalists to be adept at making thoughtful choices and resisting temptation. I tended more towards buying things because they were on sale.

***

When my father came to pick me up at the end of my freshman year of college, we spent an afternoon packing my clothes into a duffel bag to take home. As he worked his way through a dresser drawer while I tackled the closet, I could sense he was getting increasingly uncomfortable.

Finally, he cleared his throat. "I counted," he said. "You have sixty-three tank tops."

Each of those tank tops had been worn. Between dance practices, afternoons on the quad, nights out at sweaty parties, layers under sweaters, and laundry avoidance, they'd gotten me through my freshman year. And since they'd largely been sourced during lazy weekend afternoon trips to thrift stores and sale racks, I doubted I'd spent more than three or four dollars on most of them. But... still. I could see how sixty-three tank tops seemed, objectively, like too many tank tops, and I conceded as much.

In the intervening years my shopping habits, and wardrobe, matured, but I was still fundamentally the same person who at the age of eighteen ended up with sixty-three tank tops and didn't notice it was absurd because the tiny squares of fabric all fit easily into my t-shirt drawer. I liked to believe I had gotten better with time, but I had a long way to go.

***

Now I needed to try my best to put that eighteen-year-old's impulses to rest and keep my wardrobe streamlined. While I wouldn't say I achieved minimalist status, I did note that at the end of the year, there were only a handful of items that stayed with me from start to finish. A couple of black sweaters, a jean jacket, the stud earrings I never took off... I shopped often over the course of the year, but it was a different type of shopping. It was not for recreation but to replace something that I'd worn out (underwear with holes, stretched out jeans), or to adjust to a new climate (wool sweaters, a pair of shorts).

And, most shocking to me, over the course of the year, as much as I was horrified by the paltry length of my initial packing list, I didn't actually miss having more clothes to choose from. The forcing function of long-term travel was that I had to keep my wardrobe streamlined to only things that I definitely wanted to wear—not something I might at some point wear, or that might come in handy in a specific situation. Just a few things I liked enough, and that were comfortable enough, to wear constantly. The bar for buying new things was so high: we'd have to haul that item everywhere we went; there was no sticking it in the back of a closet or drawer to pull out only for the perfect occasion or when everything else was dirty.

We had KonMari'd our things before we left San Francisco, wanting to only pay to move the essentials cross-country. But after a couple months of traveling with two suitcases, I wondered why we'd kept anything at all in storage back in the US. Living out of two suitcases wasn't so bad—what on earth could I need with all the things in those boxes?

And sure enough, while my wardrobe expanded when we moved to New York and became stationary, it was nowhere near as expansive as it had been before we traveled. I found I preferred to wear the same few pairs of versatile pants repeatedly rather than switch things up. I was no longer willing to compromise on comfort after spending a year only wearing shoes in which you could reliably walk for a full day.

Upon our return from our trip, I spent less time shopping, or even coveting. I didn't go into stores or onto websites simply to browse anymore, even when there was a major sale. Instead, when I realized there was something I needed, I would go out searching for it specifically. Shopping was no longer a leisure activity, but a purposeful one.

I still had more than I needed—more than a week's worth of clothes in my closet despite easy access to a washer-dryer. But I also had way less than I'd ever had in the past—and I'd find it hard to imagine ever owning anything even approximating sixty-three tank tops again.

THE LUGGAGE

———

Meanwhile, at times our luggage would be its own character in our travels.

When our time in Rome was coming to a close, we booked train tickets to Bologna. I began to get nervous. It had nothing to do with the destination, and everything to do with the process of getting there.

Since we'd left San Francisco and arrived in Rome, we'd taken a couple of overnight trips, packing a small duffle we had on hand for such occasions and leaving the vast majority of our things in our Roman apartment.

This was the first time we would be packing everything and moving destinations wholesale. Our suitcases hadn't been stuffed when we left San Francisco, but I knew we'd made purchases during our time in Rome. Not just the things for the apartment, but clothes for Ella, a few toys, a couple things for cooler weather for Mike and me. Packing this time, I was certain, would put our suitcases to the test.

It turned out that my anxiety was misplaced. The process of packing was stressful, but ultimately we managed to zip our suitcases and head on our way. It was the process of getting to and boarding our train that nearly broke us.

We had two twenty-eight-inch rolling suitcases, a travel crib, a travel car seat, a travel stroller, and our two carry-ons stuffed with toys, bottles, and diapers. Over the coming months we'd get so good at arranging and maneuvering our luggage that when a friend or stranger offered to help, we'd urgently wave them off lest they upset our system. But six weeks in we were still learning.

***

We gathered our belongings. We managed to call an oversized taxi to take us to the train station, as the three of us and our luggage would not fit in a normal-sized car. But when it came time to board the train, we realized with horror that we'd selected a type of train service for commuters—with no luggage storage. There was space to tuck a bag between your feet, or sling something lightweight above your head, and even a hook for your suit jacket. But there wasn't even so much as an empty corner at the end of the train car for a full-sized suitcase, much less two oversized ones.

As the train pulled away, we contemplated our pile of luggage in the aisle. Italians lined up behind us, clearing their throats and gesturing. The row across the aisle from us was empty. I sat miserably in our seats with Ella, looking up how to say things like "I'm sorry" and "we didn't know" in Italian while Mike stacked our luggage precariously on the pair of empty seats, praying no one would come to claim them.

When the conductor came through, we were ready with our rehearsed Italian phrases, but he just looked at us, looked at our luggage, looked at us again, sighed and shrugged, then moved on to take the next ticket. Every time the train pulled into a station, we'd rehearse our phrases again in case someone boarded with a ticket assigned to the seats our suitcases were occupying.

Miraculously we made it to our destination without having our luggage imperialism challenged, but the stress of that train ride stayed with us, and we vowed to learn the layout of every train we booked moving forward.

WORK LIFE BALANCE

As I wrapped up my teaching job and we moved on from Rome, our travel still wasn't all leisure—at least not for me. Mike had opted not to work for the year we were traveling. He wanted to be fully present, to prioritize this experience with no distractions.

I had considered this line of thinking, but ultimately had chosen differently. In part because I had received some advice that resonated.

A few weeks before we were supposed to start our trip, I agreed to meet up with a friend of a friend at a little white-tiled, hipster-y coffee shop near our apartment in San Francisco. When I shared that I was embarking on a period of extended travel with a baby in tow, this woman said, "Oh! I know someone else who did that."

"No," I countered. *Did she understand that we were going to be gone at least six months and that we had a* baby? I pointed this out again.

"Yes," she said. "I'll introduce you to Jenna and Brandon."

And so, Mike and I ended up on a video call with this couple one evening a week before we were scheduled to leave for

Rome. I held my breath as their camera clicked on. There they were, two strangers and a toddler negotiating bedtime in their New York City apartment, recounting how they'd recently returned from a year of travel. And here we were, holding a baby, planning to embark on a year of travel, and to end our travels in my hometown of New York City, at which point our baby would be a toddler. It was like looking into the future.

"We are so happy to meet you!" they said across time and space as we adjusted the respective audio feeds on our computers. "So few people do this!"

We admitted that they were the first family we knew of, and that we were anxious to gain any insights they might have to share. Jenna and Brandon talked us through their trip.

They had left the previous summer, starting with a marathon of movement across Europe, hitting spots they'd dreamed of visiting; a new one every day or two. It was exhausting. They slowed their pace as they hit the fall, swung back through the US for the holidays and a wedding, and then went south to Latin America. They shared their highlights, lowlights, and lessons learned.

"Go slow," Brandon said. "The pacing with a baby is totally different. You can't do as much on any given stop, and if the baby is overstimulated and cranky, everyone gets cranky."

"It's a lot of time together," Jenna pointed out. "Best to trade off, each get some time to yourselves and away from each other and the baby. And some activities are just better done alone. Often we'd go to the same museum on different days rather than trying to do that together with our daughter. You can do that if you stretch out your time in a given destination."

Every past trip Mike and I had taken as a couple, we'd done everything together each day of the vacation. At that point it had never occurred to me that we wouldn't do all our sightseeing and meals together on this trip too. Though as soon as Jenna said it, the idea that we'd have to have time apart over the course of this year made total sense.

In a typical year of our lives, we spent most of our waking hours apart. Just because we were planning on spending the better part of a year traveling didn't mean we could spend 365 days in a row together and remain sane.

"Also, you might want to work a bit," Jenna said. She hadn't, and Brandon had. At first, she loved the total freedom and the chance to turn that part of her brain off. But three or four months in, she got a bit bored and was jealous of that slice of purpose in Brandon's week. "Not too much, though," she cautioned. "Not more than a day or two a week. But if you have something, I'd take it."

After a few more pieces of advice, we signed off, promising to keep in touch. I was buoyed by the conversation, elated that someone else had done this thing that we were undertaking, relieved that they'd found it to be not just possible, but fun.

***

It was Jenna's last piece of advice, however, that lodged in the back of my mind, kicking up insecurities about being a woman taking a break from the workforce, particularly so soon after becoming a mother. I had already battled my demons about stepping down as CEO so soon after giving birth. I worried it implied cause-and-effect that wasn't there. I was leaving my job to travel the world, for Pete's sake, not because leadership and motherhood were incompatible!

But the timing suggested otherwise. The perverse pervasiveness of the patriarchy seemed to dictate that I stay in a job, city, and life I wasn't happy with just to avoid sending the wrong message. I had gone to great pains to publicly tell the truth of the story of my departure from my company via news articles and blog posts just to try to avoid folks believing that my baby made me quit.

Now I was fighting another internal battle: Do I believe that I, as a woman, can take a break from the workforce and return without missing a beat? What if that break is not occasioned by but coincides with the birth of a child? The feminist in me wanted to be confident that I could do what I wanted, but the realist in me was not so sure.

As it so happened, I had two professional opportunities to consider. The first was the position teaching in Rome, the one that I would accept, grateful because it would force us to move from planning to action, and to kick off our trip at a specific time, in a specific place.

But the teaching commitment was only three weeks long. What about after that? A month or so before we left on our trip, a former colleague forwarded me another opportunity that would give me exactly what Jenna had recommended: a day a week of work.

The role itself, coaching entrepreneurs and designing portfolio support for a venture firm focused on progressive startups, was a perfect fit. The hours were good—ten per week, largely on my own schedule. And the pay was generous, which was tempting at a moment when we were staring down months of travel without income.

Yet I was deeply ambivalent.

Did I think I could take a year out of the workforce and re-enter? Yes. But would it be easier to have a part-time gig in venture capital as a steppingstone to my next role once I was back? Of course.

On the other hand, I hadn't had a break from working for over ten years, since the summer of 2007 when I quit my job a few weeks before enrolling in grad school. It's true that just before starting my company I'd been out of work for a couple months, but those had been consumed by the anxiety of job searching, before I decided to chart my own path. And from the moment I had left my company earlier that year, I was prepping for the teaching gig, writing curriculum, and compiling the syllabus. Was this my moment to finally let myself relax after what felt like a lifetime in pursuit of productivity and impact?

On the other hand, I could hear Jenna's voice in my head: *One day a week of work would have been great...* And that's what I was being offered here. Plus, I was terrified of feeling rudderless and unmoored. And while we had budgeted for a year without incomes, I knew that having an income would mean we'd feel a sense of freedom and possibility that seemed like might be key to our truly enjoying this year of travel.

Mike was torn too. He of course loved the idea of us having an income while we traveled. But if I was working, that would also mean extra childcare for him, and less family time for all of us.

But even this calculus was complex. Before Ella was born, we had discussed our intention to split childcare responsibilities fifty-fifty. But in order to keep our healthcare coverage active, Mike had ended up working right up until the time we left the country, so he had not yet had the chance to be the primary parent.

As Ella was breastfeeding less, the chance to ensure that Mike had a period where he was spending more time on childcare than I was seemed like a worthwhile exercise—a chance to lay a foundation for balance in the next twenty years of our marriage.

After talking it over with Mike, I decided to take the job. The notion of continuity on my resume, continuing to build my network, and calming the demons inside that said I was worthless unless I was working all factored in—but in the end what carried the day was the money.

Between the teaching gig and the consulting gig, plus a couple other projects I ended up taking over the course of the year, my income ended up covering the cost of our trip. For this stretch of time, I'd be the breadwinner—not just primary, but only. Patriarchy be damned.

WORKING WITHOUT
INFRASTRUCTURE

———

I ended up enjoying my consulting work throughout the year we traveled. In some ways, like the teaching gig at the university, it was a balm to the soul after such a fraught final stretch with my own company; a reminder that work could be work, that I could end a day feeling useful and accomplished, rather than inadequate and drained.

In this way my teaching and consulting served like rebound relationships. I knew they weren't going anywhere long term, but they reminded me of what work could be. I could choose to do what was difficult for me—starting something new, running a change management process, leaning into and leading deep conversations around race and equity— or I could choose to do something else. I had options. This would serve me well when we returned from our travels and I was trying to figure out what to do next.

It was difficult at the time, however. Mike and I had aligned on the idea that a couple times a week we'd trade off time with Ella so that the other person could have some solo time. The expectation was that this would allow each of us to see some sights, eat at some restaurants, and generally partake in a few activities that were not baby-friendly.

But my working complicated things a bit. The fact that I had first teaching and then consulting to integrate into this schedule meant that while Mike's off-days were spent going to museums and drinking wine with lunch, at least some of mine were spent hunched over a laptop and doing video calls with colleagues back in the States. As much as I did enjoy the work, I had to admit that I hated the obligation, and the fact that it meant Mike and I were constantly negotiating how much time I needed to work versus what time we could be together.

Mike taking more Ella-time didn't fully solve the problem. While it gave me more time to explore on my own, it took away from time we could spend exploring together as a family. As a result, my working meant I always had to choose whether being alone and at leisure or being with Mike and Ella and at leisure was more valuable to me, rather than getting to fully enjoy both.

I knew this predicament was not foreign to working parents, but it was new to me given how soon we had embarked on this trip after Ella was born. And unlike in San Francisco where I hadn't felt much urge to explore after a decade of residency, this conundrum felt to me to be in stark relief when set against so many different destinations over the course of our trip. I'd spend more than one day that year on a conference call while staring wistfully out the window, wondering if I'd made the right choice in deciding to work at all.

Then, about six months into our trip, there was one destination where I got a glimpse of what it would be like to have infrastructure to support my working.

***

On our first full day in Madrid, on a rainy spring morning in April, I brought Ella to a playgroup. It was in a little storefront not far from our apartment. After forty-five minutes of music ending with a grand finale of a bubble machine, we wrapped up. As I was packing up Ella's things, the woman who owned the place started chatting with me, asking what brought us to town.

I launched into my standard answer: "We're traveling for a year... Yes, with a baby..."

"Ah!" she said. "Well I was going to say that we use these desks up front for coworking. We have a *monitora* who can watch up to four babies at a time. But it sounds like you're not working..."

"I am working!" I proclaimed, and promptly booked three two-hour sessions over the course of the week.

For once, Mike could explore and I could work, and someone else could watch Ella! Then on my days without Ella, I could simply relax into a cup of coffee or a glass of wine or play at being a tourist. It was a relief.

Mike and I got better with time at figuring out a cadence of trading off sightseeing and watching Ella, plus spending time together. But it would never change the fact that I envied Mike's not having something he had to do at all times hanging over his head.

On the other hand, I couldn't be sure that, without this sense of purpose and obligation, I wouldn't have begun to feel anxious and directionless. Would I have been able to enjoy our trip if our bank balance had been dropping daily rather than remaining steady? If I had been worried about my ability to reenter the workforce upon our return? I don't know.

Ultimately I had to resign myself to the fact that I'd never know whether a choice to not work would have felt like a joyous one or a mistake.

YOU HAVE ONE FRIEND

———

One of the things I was most nervous about as we prepared for our year of travel was the prospect of having no friends—at least no friends that I could see on any regular basis. Or, to be more precise, I was nervous about the prospect of having exactly one friend: Mike. (I didn't think Ella, unable to speak, should count.)

Mike and I met in law school. At the beginning of our relationship, we were constantly surrounded by mutual friends.

When he and I started hanging out in the fall of our first year, we and two of our friends formed something we called the Bitterness Brigade, which was basically us being cranky and drinking happy-hour wine six days a week. (The truth is, Mike wasn't bitter. He loved school. But he was also coming to love me and is a critic by nature, so it wasn't hard for him to blend in.)

While we spent plenty of time together just the two of us, in those early days we rarely went on anything that could be considered a date—our interwoven social circles and the communal nature of graduate school made hanging out in groups the most natural way to spend an evening.

As time and our relationship progressed, we spent more time together by ourselves—nights out, trips, and eventually, living together. But still, our mutual friends were never far away.

We got married a year after graduation. Leading up to the wedding, I was living in Los Angeles, working at a tech startup as a VP. Mike was in San Francisco, an associate at a law firm. At the time we liked both cities, we had friends in both places, and we weren't sure where to land. So, we made it simple: whoever's job was winning, the other person would move to join them.

Mike wasn't in his forever-job, that was for sure. He didn't love working at a law firm, but he was surrounded by friends there and it paid the bills—including the very substantial student loan bills. And by the summer of 2011, as we counted down towards our wedding, it was pretty clear that my job was losing. The company I was at was pivoting, and it looked like a pivot to the bottom of the ocean. I jumped ship and moved back up to San Francisco.

Typically, the honeymoon phase is considered a high point in married life, but this turned out to be the opposite for us. Our honeymoon itself was pretty spectacular: a splurge trip to Tanzania funded via our registry during which, in the perfect combination of romantic and hilarious, Mike saved me from a baboon. But things took a turn for the worse upon our return.

Through a combination of bad planning and frugality, we ended up on a forty-hour, four-flight journey from Zanzibar to San Francisco, both sick on the way back, and exhausted once home. Mike's boss at the law firm (unlimited vacation days, but damned if you try to take them) told him to come in the next day. And that, my friends, was the last time I saw my husband in 2011.

I sat in my pajamas in our tiny Chinatown apartment scouring job boards, sending off my resume into a hundred black holes never to get a reply. Mike worked ninety-hour weeks and moved like a zombie through his few hours of free time on the weekends.

With Mike stuck at work and me stuck at home, those early months of marriage were bad. They were made worse by the fact that I had few friends in San Francisco. Most of my friends from grad school had moved away. I was lonely and anxious, haunted by a voice in my head that said I had moved for a man and this is what I got.

Over the years I'd make new friends, and a few old ones would move back. But as someone who had prided herself on cultivating and maintaining deep friendships, those early days in San Francisco when most of my loved ones were distant left scars.

I knew what it felt like to not have any friends around besides Mike, and I didn't like it. So, when we embarked on our trip, despite the fact that the better part of a decade had passed between that rocky start to our marriage and the impending start of our trip, I was wary of the prospect of having only one friend for the upcoming year.

Of course, we wouldn't have the issue of Mike being consumed with work. In fact, our challenge would be the opposite. We wouldn't be pulled away from one another; we would be pushed together. What pressures would it put on our relationship to be with each other, and only each other, for so much of the time, for a year?

100 DATE NIGHTS

Once we were on our year of travel, I got connected with a handful of other families, friends of friends, who had done something similar. I spoke on the phone to a few of the women with whom I was put in touch, and in each case asked whether they thought their year abroad had altered their relationship with their spouse and, if so, how?

The answer was surprisingly uniform. The time spent traveling had made their partnership feel more "solid." That was the word I heard over and over. And by the end of the trip, I would realize how much it resonated with me and my experience, too.

"We just ended up navigating so many different situations together," one woman said. "It felt like we were a team."

Mike and I had been together for a long time before we embarked on this trip. But the difference between living intersecting lives, even intertwined lives, and living lives in near total synchronicity was profound.

In our typical lives, we spent the vast majority of our time apart: working at our respective offices, pursuing different hobbies, hanging out with separate friends in some portion of our free time.

On this trip, we spent the vast majority of our time together. Each day, we tackled challenges together. Some of these were mundane, like figuring out where to grocery shop, or navigating public transit in a new city and language. But many were more consequential, like navigating illness and medical care in a foreign system and culture.

And then there was the sheer quantity of decisions we needed to make together during our year abroad. Decisions that typically a couple makes once in a while, like how much to spend on rent when you move apartments, we made once a week. Over the course of our year of travel we made what felt like a decade of decisions together. From simple ones like whether or where to stop for lunch, to more complex ones, like whether and when we felt comfortable leaving our child with a stranger in a place where we were strangers ourselves.

Mike and I—both strong-willed, opinionated, and prone to thinking we're definitely, 100% right—had clashed a thousand times in the prior ten years, and we'd continue to clash on our trip on many occasions. But the sheer volume and frequency of shared decision-making, the relentlessness of navigating challenging, unfamiliar situations together day in and day out, created a kind of rhythm in our relationship, a smoothing of the rough edges, that would persist upon our return.

Months later, after our travels, I would be struck by how simple it was for us to make major decisions together. Where in New York City to live, which apartment to rent, what childcare arrangement we wanted for Ella, whether to buy a house and if so which one... Decisions that could easily have been fraught were not. It would be easy to think that we just had the same ideas about these things independently, that our thinking happened to align. But that would be oversimplifying the situation.

Over the course of our time abroad, we lived in forty-eight different cities and towns, and slept in forty-eight different apartments and hotel rooms. Through that experience, and the forty-eight decisions that it required, we knew a *lot* about what we each valued, and what we collectively valued, in a place to live, be it the physical characteristics or the neighborhood it is in. So, when it was time to consider buying a home, we were on the same page.

Similarly, we'd explored both our risk tolerance around childcare, and our prioritization of it while we traveled. We had discussed the advantages of Ella spending so much time with her parents and other adult caregivers, and the drawbacks. So, we were clear on what we wanted for Ella when we returned. And on what we wanted for our family (and our sanity) when that childcare plan was upended at the start of the coronavirus pandemic.

The intensity of our time together over the year was a boon for our relationship in many ways, but it could be challenging as we went through it. "How was your day?" became a farcical question. Most days we were side by side and knew how our collective day was going as we progressed through it.

We went on nearly one hundred "dates" over the course of our travels. That is, we took advantage of childcare to do nearly one hundred things together as a couple—meals mostly, but drinks, movies, museums, walks through unfamiliar neighborhoods… even a night at the symphony. There were many times where we went through an entire day together, left Ella with a babysitter, and then went out together again to share a cocktail.

In those cases, we didn't have much news to share. We hadn't experienced different things over the course of the day, we hadn't spoken to anyone whom the other person hadn't also spoken to, and we lacked new stories to bring to the table. Instead of simply recounting the recent past to make conversation, we were forced to discuss the present and the future, or more abstract things like priorities, hopes, and dreams. Or to be comfortable with companionable silence.

I imagined this might be what it felt like to be married for many years. A sort of comfortable inevitability to our time together, a sense of companionship. It took a while to settle into it, and it was strange to experience it at a moment when our lives were in the midst of such transition.

But it was one of the outcomes of the trip for which, upon our return, I was most grateful. When, six months after our trip, just as we'd settled back into intersecting lives, COVID forced us to suddenly revert to spending nearly all our time together again, we didn't get on each other's nerves. We were used to navigating long stretches of being one another's only adult companion. With all the stress of the pandemic, it was a relief at least to not be stressing each other out. It felt ironic that months on end of travel would be preparation for months on end of being homebound, but I was thankful for the ways in which it was.

TRAVELING VS VACATIONING

———

When we first started telling people that we were embarking on a year of travel, a number of friends and family said they'd like to join us for a stretch. On the one hand, we were thrilled to have company and relieved that we would get to see the people we loved and cared about over the course of our year abroad.

On the other hand, the logistics of aligning our travels with the travel plans of others were tricky. And beyond that, the experience of trying to sync up the day-to-day cadence of our travel—our default pacing that would sustain us for more than 300 days on the road—with the cadence of our vacationing friends, for whom this was often their big trip of the year, was difficult.

At one point in our planning, I spoke to a friend who had spent a few months in Costa Rica after having her second child. She and her wife had rented a large house with extra bedrooms in it and sent around a sign-up sheet to their closest family and friends. It wasn't long into our trip before I saw the wisdom of their approach.

We basically did the opposite. We met up with twenty-five people over the course of our time spent traveling, in eleven distinct groupings, on fourteen separate occasions (my parents and Mike's mom came more than once). In the end, about a third of our time spent traveling would be with other people.

There were huge advantages to traveling with friends and family. When people arrived, they were on vacation, and brought a buzzy energy with them that helped reinvigorate us. We had other adults to talk to, in our language, which was not a given depending on what country we were in at the time. We had more motivation to push ourselves to see sights and wander farther from our home base, which could feel daunting and draining with a baby in tow.

If our visitors had kids, Ella had a playmate for a time. And if they didn't, we had an extra set of hands around, someone for whom bouncing a baby or building a block tower was a novelty.

But for all the positives, there were major downsides, too. One of the hardest pieces of traveling with others was trying to contort our own travel schedule to match up with our guests' preferences. Since we were not planning too far ahead for ourselves, usually others' vacations would end up serving as an anchor in our future planning.

Once we'd aligned on when and where we were meeting up and when and where we were parting ways, there were still challenges to plotting out the time we'd be spending together. Folks' desired pacing of their trip on a one- to two-week vacation was wildly different than our desired pacing on a year-long journey. Visitors often wanted to do a night or two in a given location and were willing to cover great distances in between destinations to squeeze in sights they were curious about.

We, on the other hand, preferred to spend a week or more in a given destination and were hesitant to ever travel more than three hours in a day, timed carefully with Ella's nap for maximum palatability.

When traveling with my brother and his girlfriend in December, we moved destinations every two nights so as to see more of Belgium—and this was only after negotiating away from a schedule that would have had us moving destinations every day. Even that proved to be too much.

When friends on their babymoon in July proposed a similar schedule moving through Scandinavia, we'd learned our lesson. We arrived early in Bergen to give ourselves a couple extra days to get settled before they arrived, then went together to Oslo. When they jumped to Copenhagen twenty-four hours later, we remained in Oslo, and met them three days later in Stockholm. These choices weren't easy; both Mike and I really wanted to go to Denmark, and we were so close to it! But we knew that we wouldn't be able to enjoy the city with Ella at that pace, and that pushing ourselves too hard would take away from our enjoyment of the other destinations, too.

Ultimately, even with these accommodations, we figured out that traveling with others required not just a particular cadence while it was going on, but also breaks in between guests. We could sustain that vacation pacing for a week or so, but then needed time to slow down afterwards.

LAST MINUTE
TRAVEL FOR THE
NON-SPONTANEOUS

———

When coordinating our travel with others, the process of choosing destinations was relatively straightforward, as our travel companions tended to have ideas about where they wanted to go. But for us, picking nearly a year's worth of destinations provided its own challenges and opportunities.

Typically, when we were planning prior vacations, we chose where to travel based on things we'd read or things we'd heard from friends. With only relatively short stretches of time allocated for those sorts of trips, we wanted to minimize the risk of choosing somewhere we wouldn't enjoy, so clear recommendations and some level of consensus felt wise.

With such a long stretch of time ahead of us on this trip, we decided to relax our standards a bit. What if we picked a place because something about it piqued our interest, rather than because it had been "vetted" by travel sites and our friend group? After all, what was the worst that could happen? On a vacation of a week or two, a mis-picked destination could drag down the quality of the whole trip. On an adventure spanning a year, a few days in a dud of a location didn't seem like it would make much difference at all.

There were certainly a few duds on our trip but by and large this thinking, and the more off-beat destinations it led us to choose, turned out to lead to some of our most memorable travel experiences—from sheep farms to ghost towns to stargazing hotspots.

***

This type of more relaxed destination picking didn't come naturally to me. And it wasn't just the locations we were relaxed about; the timing of our decision-making on this trip was wildly different than what I was used to, too. Often we booked transportation or lodging just a few days in advance. Given how quickly we embraced this last-minute planning, it would be easy to think that it came naturally to us, but it didn't.

In my day-to-day life, I had never been particularly spontaneous. I relished having plans and gained great solace from feeling in control of my schedule and my time. While I got bored easily and had never been attracted to routine, I craved and was comforted by predictability.

As such, for my whole adult life, my vacations had always been pre-planned. Not just the flights and the number of days in each location, but where we were staying and often what we were doing and where we were eating on any given day. My philosophy was: If you have a plan in place, you can always change it; but without one you're likely to miss out on things or waste the day. I could see how this would be a stressful way to approach a vacation for some, but for me, doing the planning in advance let me relax into the experiences as they came.

This year of travel broke all my normal habits.

Mike and I discussed it in advance and decided that we didn't want to set an end date for our trip before we left. We figured if we kept our expenses low, we could afford to travel for about a year, so that was our outer limit. But we had no idea how Ella would react to a nomadic lifestyle as she grew, and whether what sounded like an adventure of a lifetime on paper would end up feeling like a slog in reality. We were set to leave the US on September 30, and it didn't seem impossible that we'd be ready to come home by that same Christmas.

We decided that if we weren't sure on an end date, it made sense to play most of the trip by ear. We'd sketch a general arc but let the time when we had guests joining us on our travels be the only times we'd commit to planning far in advance. We wouldn't overcommit, just in case we needed to bail. The rest of the time we'd make sure we had a place to sleep a few days before we needed it, but perhaps not much more than that.

This was a massive departure from my typical way of traveling—and living—and I was looking forward to it. That's because, while it wasn't my normal way of operating, I did know what it was like to live in the moment, because I had done it exactly one time.

***

Fall of 2014, Mike and I took a vacation to France. We had ended up landing on France sort of by accident, tacking personal travel on to work travel, so I was looking forward to the time away but not especially excited about the destination. And, coming off a particularly difficult stretch at work, I hadn't had much time to plan the details of the trip. So, I decided to try something new.

On this trip, whenever we were faced with a choice—what to do that day, where to eat, whether to stop for a coffee now or later—I would make the decision by asking myself simply: *Would this make me happy right now?* Rather than try to optimize the trip or to defer satisfaction in the name of being responsible, I would focus on collecting small moments of small pleasures.

Should I buy a croissant from this bakery? What if I hadn't researched the best bakeries in the neighborhood we were in at that moment? Rather than worry if this was the best croissant available, or that if I had this croissant I should later forgo cheese lest the day's calorie count get too high, I would simply ask: *Would eating this croissant make me happy right now?* (The answer was always yes.)

I didn't worry about what we *should* do, what I *should* eat, *should, should, should*. I didn't try to optimize my vacation, or my life—I simply tried to optimize each moment when a choice came up.

That was an excellent vacation.

When I remembered that experience, I looked forward to an under-planned year of travel.

WHEN IN ITALY, FOLLOW YOUR STOMACH

———

We left the US with only two things set: our one-way flights to Italy, and our six weeks of student housing in Rome. For the first month, I was busy at the university with my teaching, so we simply relished being in Rome, where there was an endless stream of things to do, see, and eat. But eventually, in early November, our time in Rome drew to a close, and our first travel choices needed to be made.

We made plans to meet Mike's mother towards the end of November in Milan, which meant we had about two weeks to get from Rome to Milan. But where to go in between? The options seemed nearly endless.

One evening in our apartment in Rome, Mike and I decided to watch an episode of the newly released travel and cooking show *Salt Fat Acid Heat* in which chef Samin Nosrat explores different elements of flavor. We'd been told the "Fat" episode took place in Italy.

As we watched Samin eat her way through the middle of Italy, we turned to each other, practically salivating. She had just finished a visit to a parmesan factory outside Parma, in the region of Emilia-Romagna. It was north of us, between Rome and Milan.

"Should we... go there?" Mike asked me.

What better way to choose our route than by our stomachs? He did some quick searching online and found that you didn't have to be a celebrity chef to visit the home of the cheese of the *vacche rosse*. For five euros apiece, we could go on the same tour that had been filmed for the special.

Mike filled out the contact form, and a few days later we were booked. We built the next segment of our trip around our cheese tour.

We learned that this region was also home to some of the best cured meats in Italy. After some reflection on the fact that the red cows played a different role in the production of cheeses than black pigs played in the production of cured meats, we decided that if we were willing to eat the prosciutto, we should be willing to meet the prosciutto. Mike found a place we could tour that produced artisanal prosciutto from their own farm, and our next destination was chosen.

We also reasoned that if we were passing so close to Modena, we must spend some time learning about balsamic. We booked three nights in an *agriturismo*, a boutique hotel on a working vineyard that produced its own barrel-aged vinegar.

With that, we had our schedule.

***

Our stomachs led us in Italy, but we pursued other goals in other countries. In December we spent two weeks in Amsterdam because I had read an article on an obscure mommy blog about *kindercafes*—coffee shops with indoor play areas for toddlers. Since the weather was turning and playgrounds were no longer a suitable way to pass much time, the idea of sipping a latte while Ella tumbled around freely was appealing enough that we booked our flights.

When our friends invited us to stay with them in their house on the Isle of Skye for New Year's, we planned three dark and dramatic weeks in Scotland split between the rural lochs and Edinburgh's medieval charms.

When we realized we would have a few extra days in June between a beach vacation with friends in French Basque country and a meetup with my parents on the craggy coast of Western Ireland, we pictured the rolling hills of the Irish countryside. We found a working farm a few hours from the Dublin airport where the reviews mentioned that everything about the breakfast from the eggs to the yogurt to the apple juice was made in-house from farm ingredients.

It was always a joy to share our trip with others, and to go to our friends' dream destinations alongside them. But over the course of the year I'd shock myself by coming to prefer the laissez faire planning and relaxed pacing of our solo family time over the structure, rigidity, and greatest-hits-style planning of co-traveling—the very same style I used to embrace.

Throughout our trip we often mused whether long-term travel had ruined short-term vacations for us. Would we ever again be able to pop from destination to destination, packing in sights, milking our days until we were exhausted? Or would we maintain this slow pace only to find ourselves flying halfway around the world to spend lazy mornings at coffee shops and playgrounds not so different from a weekend at home? Was there a middle ground?

When it came time to schedule our first vacation after returning from our travels, we decided to pick a destination we'd already been to and had loved: Mexico City. We figured this would relieve some pressure to sightsee, allowing us to focus only on the few key tourist attractions we'd missed the first time around. We had a connection through which we found a babysitter, which would enable Mike and me to do those sights together—but without Ella. This way, we wouldn't have to trade off, and during family time we could prioritize relaxing with street tacos and churros in parks, an activity more likely to appeal to all three of us.

As it so happened, none of this came to fruition. Our trip was scheduled for April 2020, and by then we were in full pandemic lockdown. I didn't even have to cancel our flights—the airline did it for us. All of our hard-won travel lessons would end up lying dormant, waiting for the day in which we could dust them off and put them to the test all over again, and leaving the question of how our trip would impact our future travel as a matter of speculation.

BABY STEPS

———

In November, following our stomachs, we continued our way north through Italy. We left Bologna, where we had reveled in the local specials like mortadella and tortellini, to spend some time in the outskirts of Modena.

We visited a barn where two men continued their family tradition of producing balsamic; their oldest barrel was one hundred years old, the vinegar syrupy and condensed. We made good on our plan to visit the parmesan factory, buying hunks of cheese several years old that we'd carry with us as Christmas gifts. We stood in a room that looked like the stacks in a university library, but on each shelf hung a haunch of prosciutto.

Then, after two weeks in the countryside, we dropped our car by the train station in Parma, where we'd spend Thanksgiving.

***

Two days into our week in Parma, just as Ella turned ten months old, she pulled herself up to stand against the sofa in our rental apartment and set her sights on a toy across the room. With great determination, she turned herself towards her target, and set off: *step, step.* Then she toppled over and began to crawl.

Mike and I stared at each other. *She walked!* Ella took her first steps at a moment when we both happened to be looking at her.

That night, after she was asleep, we lay stretched out on the couch staring at the ceiling, sipping wine, and wondering if we'd have seen those first steps if we'd stayed back in San Francisco, if we'd both been working, out of the house fifty hours a week or more. It was possible, of course—but what were the odds?

Spending this much uninterrupted time together was an unintended consequence of taking this trip. We were spending almost all our waking hours together. In fact, I realized one day with a shock, we were basically stay-at-home parents—except without the staying, or the home.

This had never been a goal or desire of mine. I had always derived so much of my identity and meaning from work, that being a stay at home mother, even for a stretch, was never a notion I entertained. Of course, I was working a bit on this trip—the teaching gig in Rome, the consulting gig with the venture firm—but it was only a few hours per week, and often in evenings or during nap times. For the most part, during many of my waking hours, I was parenting.

The strange thing is, the chance to spend more time together as a family was not really part of the calculus when we decided to travel. In fact, in many ways we took this trip in spite of Ella. Mike and I had wanted this chance at exploration for ourselves. Ella was merely along for the ride.

And while we knew that spending so much time with her parents was probably, on balance, a good thing for her, we did fret a bit about her not getting enough time with extended family and kids her age. We hoped this trip would build up her adaptability and resilience, but knew that would come at the cost of her building bonds with grandparents and learning the basics of how to share.

Throughout all the ambivalence, we hung on to one idea: this year is a privilege. It's a privilege to get to choose family over work and exploration over obligation. It's a privilege to have the chance to watch Ella's development, and for her to get so much of our attention.

***

A few months later I'd head back to the US for a couple days on a work trip, leaving Mike and Ella behind. I'd sit on the plane by myself: no Mike, no Ella, just me. And it would feel weird. I reveled in the moments to myself, but I was uneasy. Not because we were apart, but because being apart was so foreign. That fact in and of itself was unsettling—because spending time apart, eight to ten hours a day not to mention a few nights away here and there—wouldn't be weird in a few months when we were back in the US, with jobs, and regular lives.

As I recalled Ella's glee, how proud she was of herself after taking those first baby steps, I wondered: *Have we spoiled ourselves beyond redemption in some way with this chance to spend so much time together as a family?*

Not that it was universally amazing to spend all your time with the same two people, of course, particularly when one of them can't talk. But it was experiencing this extreme that highlighted the opposite extreme of how divergent our lives tend to be in a given day from those of our loved ones.

I'd marvel at this change when we finally landed in New York and started commuting to two offices and daycare. I'd marvel at it again when a global pandemic closed all three of those spaces and forced us all back together in our home.

But that was all a ways off. At the time I simply used the occasion of Ella's first steps to remind myself to feel lucky—not just for the chance to travel, but for the chance to be present with my travel companions, too.

ON TO AMSTERDAM

Of course, as important as the time together was, alone time was valuable as well. It was hard to come by when we were traveling with visitors, so we scheduled it in when we were on stretches of traveling by ourselves.

In early December, after traveling with Mike's mother for our last week in Italy, we flew up to Amsterdam. We had two weeks there just the three of us before my brother and his girlfriend would join for a hectic stretch that took us through Christmas with my parents and then New Year's and early January with friends. This was to be our last stretch just the three of us for about a month. As a result, we divided up a lot of the time in Amsterdam and hired several wonderful babysitters, and I had multiple afternoons to myself.

I immediately fell in love with Amsterdam. Some of the initial shine was definitely the varied cuisine; the chance to eat several types of Asian food after two months of Italian flavors was heaven. But what really did it for me were those canals.

The downtown area was beautiful. Despite the cold, I never got tired of walking the quaint narrow streets and crossing bridges over lazily flowing canals. There was a light installation that dotted some of the main canals for the holidays, so around 4:00 p.m. as it started to get dark, the lights would twinkle on, and it was worth bundling up and taking a walk all over again for the new views.

Even though the days were gray and often a bit rainy, the daylight hours were short, there were no leaves on the trees, and the only tulips I saw were in a museum, Amsterdam was still astoundingly picturesque.

Also, after being in Italy for so long, Amsterdam felt amazingly culturally accessible. For one, there were black and brown people all around, walking down the street, in the restaurants and cafes and museums, and they were a mix of recent immigrants and Netherlands-born Dutch. In Italy, the majority of the black people we saw were young, male African immigrants begging on the street. Our experience was quite segregated, and it wasn't until we were in Amsterdam that I realized how much I missed the type of racial mixing I was accustomed to in the United States, imperfections and all.

When I walked into a shop in Amsterdam, the shopkeeper would start speaking to me in Dutch. And if Ella and I met someone in English at a cafe, they might address me in Dutch ten minutes later, or assume I understood when their child said something to me in Dutch. I kept having to clarify that I only spoke English. It was a fascinating change after being in Italy where, though I did speak the language a little, I always felt like I was seen as the foreigner that I was. In Amsterdam I had no clue what people were saying to me, but they assumed I might live just down the street.

***

That said, it wasn't all idyllic. We happened to be in Amsterdam for one of the city's annual festivals, the *Sinterklaas* parade. A friend of a friend told us *Sinterklaas*, who was like the Dutch version of Santa Claus, would be making an appearance alongside the canals in her neighborhood, and all the local school children had the morning off to see him. She invited us to join her.

In doing a bit of research about what to expect, we came across a description of Sinterklaas's companion *Zwarte Piet*, or Black Peter, who was traditionally depicted by someone in blackface.

"Oh no, Mike," I said, looking up from my laptop when I came across the imagery and the articles describing the controversy. "We are in that episode of *The Office* where Dwight is Belsnickel."

By December 2018, Amsterdam was already deep in a national debate about whether *Zwarte Piet* had a place in contemporary holiday celebrations. To modernize the character, the decision had been made that he would no longer appear in blackface, but rather would be marked with a bit of soot, presumably left from his work delivering gifts down chimneys.

As we strolled the canals waiting for Sinterklaas to appear, we walked by several children with black smudged on their faces in *Zwarte Piet*'s honor. I wondered what the black and brown Dutch moms and dads ushering their kids through the crowds thought of this, but it didn't seem an appropriate question for a stranger.

My whole life in San Francisco was oriented around interrogating issues of race. Trying to get people to see inequities and biases in our systems and cultures. If the same debate had been happening in the US, I would have felt an obligation to comment publicly, to try to shape it through the lens of equity.

Now I was simply a tourist to it. And so, after *Sinterklaas* made his appearance at the parade, rather than analyzing the cultural implications of the event, Mike and Ella and I went to get a morning slice of Dutch apple pie.

THE BELLS TOLL FOR ME

———

When my brother Jonathan and his girlfriend Alison arrived to meet us in Amsterdam, we moved to an apartment that could accommodate us all. This kicked off two weeks we'd spend with them, including meeting up with my parents in Paris a few days before Christmas to celebrate the holiday.

While it was wonderful to see family, we had planned much of this stretch of travel right at the start of our trip, and without much experience under our belt, and we had misjudged our ability to keep up with their kid-less pacing. We were paying for it.

By the time we arrived in Bruges after a long day on trains and in taxis, the adults were eager to get out and stretch our legs and get our bearings. But Ella was tired of being confined to a baby carrier for most of the day, couldn't care less about seeing the sights, and all she wanted to explore was her toys. We knew if we packed her right up again and brought her out into the cold, she'd end up cranky, making us cranky, and so there was no point. Only one of us could go.

Mike took one look at me, exhausted from the day, and desperately in need of a break, and offered to stay back at the apartment with Ella. I accepted gratefully and headed out with Jonathan and Alison to the medieval center of Bruges to visit the bell tower.

***

Jonathan, Alison, and I bought tickets to climb the tower just before it closed at sundown. As we made our way up the winding flights, pausing at the different landings to catch our breath, see the view, and explore the exhibits along the way, we got separated. Suddenly I found myself a few stories up in the air, in an 800-year-old bell tower, in a moment of sudden solitude.

As I climbed the winding steps of the bell tower, I relished this unexpected, accidental moment of being alone.

I reached a landing, and peered out a small round window, breathing the wintry air. I took my cell phone out to snap a photo of the medieval town laid out below, and caught sight of the time. In a few minutes, the bell tower would close for the day, but before it did, the bells would toll the hour. I raced up the last few flights to the belfry, arriving just as the carillon bells began to chime. The belfry was empty, and I was alone with the giant bells.

Christmas had always been my favorite time of the year—the lights, the traditions, the warmth and coziness. I looked down over Bruges, a city that must have inspired every gingerbread house, as twilight set in and the Christmas lights twinkled on. Being completely surrounded by the overwhelming, up-close tones and vibrations of the song of the bells of the thirteenth century bell tower… it was magical.

After a minute, a few other tourists reached the belfry, panting from their race to catch the show from its center. I moved out of their way, sat on the floor in a corner and closed my eyes, preferring to preserve the feeling of being alone.

I let the stress of the travel day melt away. I took a deep breath and paused the never-ending narrative that came along with co-traveling. I stopped caring what anyone else wanted to do, or didn't want to do, or what they needed, or whether we had enough milk and diapers. I tapped into the deep gratitude I felt for having the opportunity to do this crazy trip.

We were lucky to be able to afford it. We were lucky to be healthy enough to make the journey. I was damn lucky to have a spouse who thought it was just as necessary an adventure as I did. It was at times tiring, and it was hard, but life is at times tiring, and life is hard. And this was a version of hard I had chosen, and I was privileged to be able to choose.

On a vacation, it is possible to leave normal stresses behind with the promise to pick them up again a week or two later, upon return. On an extended trip like this one, there was no out-of-office option. Every stressor followed us. There was no taking a break from responsibilities for a year. Every insecurity, every demon was there, nagging, threatening to pull me out of the moment and to cause me to miss what was beautiful.

But at that moment the bells were so loud I couldn't hear the demons or the doubts. They drowned out the irritations and insecurities.

As the final tones faded away, I realized I had been crying.

I dried my eyes and got up. The other tourists were starting down the winding stairs. I took a long look out the window at the fairytale scene. And then I descended to rendezvous with my fellow travelers in the town square below.

***

When Mike and Ella joined us, I was feeling refreshed. The center market square of Bruges had been taken over by a large Christmas market, with strands of lights, festive music, and vendors selling spit-roasted sausages, potatoes raclette, and holiday trinkets. Mike, Ella, Jonathan, Alison, and I walked the perimeter, sipping mulled wine, and soaking up the festive atmosphere. We grabbed some food and claimed a spot at a table in the middle of the market, stamping our feet to stay warm.

We were chatting and drinking, when a flock of seagulls flew by, squawking, overhead. Ella looked up.

"BUHD!" she shouted.

"WHAT?!" I shouted in return.

Her first steps in Parma, her first word in Bruges. I only had vague memories of Ella's first smile, tooth, solid food, her first time sitting, crawling, standing—all those things took place in our San Francisco apartment, the same backdrop causing days and dates to blur. But I would always remember every first that happened on our trip, each unique backdrop throwing the milestone into relief.

We cheered and toasted, and it was good.

BABY MUSIC CLASS

———

Every time we booked ourselves into a new city, I'd scour the web and social media for mommy blogs and groups in an effort to track down kid-friendly activities. During my one-on-one time with Ella, I much preferred to have a structured activity to do as an anchor, and I liked the novelty of dropping into this mundane parenting ritual in a new culture and seeing what it was like. It was an easy way to indulge in a brief fantasy that we weren't nomads at all, but rather residents of whatever city we were in.

Back in San Francisco, Ella and I had done mommy and me yoga together. She would lie under me on the mat while I did downward dogs and warrior poses above her. When she, or one of the other babies in the class, would get too fussy or start to cry, the instructor would scoop her up and bounce her around the room while providing the next round of postures and instructions and corrections. There was a strict "no talking" rule, but about a third of the class was breastfeeding at any given time.

The other class Ella attended before we left on our trip, Mike and I brought her to together. It was designed to teach parents how to care for their child with respect, to provide healthy boundaries and encouragement, and to interact and intervene only in ways that were productive, loving, and necessary. I have no idea if Ella had fun in these classes, I was so focused on being a good student in this weird ritual of performative parenting.

Both of these classes felt culturally spot on for the San Francisco Bay Area, the culture I'd been immersed in for the better part of a decade.

As we traveled, however, I soon discovered that the hardest part about going to all these different mom's groups, play groups, and music classes in different countries was not finding them or securing a spot, but figuring out the culture of parenting in these classes when the context was foreign. I always had a moment upon arrival of trying to read the room. What were the other parents doing? Where were they standing or sitting, and where was that in relation to their child? Were they observing, or corralling, or containing? Were they focused on their child, or chatting with one another?

The norms were different depending on the culture, the city—perhaps even the class—and I didn't know what they were going to be in advance. And since they were norms, not rules, often no one would explicitly say what was acceptable behavior and what was not.

In Rome, after my eye-opening encounter with an Italian moms' group where the norm was to share openly about your sex life, I had tracked down a couple of English-speaking playgroups to bring Ella to instead. These mostly consisted of informal chatting, apple slices, and an occasional group song.

In Amsterdam, I brought Ella to a class where the instructor sat on the floor with her guitar, surrounded by a pile of musical instruments. The children toddled around, picking up what interested them, sitting where they pleased, banging and shaking. The parents remained at the perimeter, singing and clapping along. At one point a child began strumming the teacher's guitar along with her. This was met with an encouraging smile.

In Edinburgh, I found a music class a few blocks from our apartment that took place in the back room of a local cafe. I learned the hard way that, at this music class, you were not to touch anything that wasn't explicitly offered to you. The norm was to sit still in a circle and sing along in an orderly fashion until you were given permission to dance, which happened twice in the hour. Each upcoming song was signaled by the presentation of a specific toy—which you were not to touch.

The Scottish kids seemed to be having a great time. Ella, who was a year old, and wanted to investigate her surroundings, not sit in her mom's lap for a concert, was confused by the restrictions.

Having come most recently from the Dutch class where the kids were little explorers, wandering the room and experimenting with the sounds different instruments made, this was a stark contrast. I had no vantage point from which to see whether this class was typical in Edinburgh any more than I did whether the one in Amsterdam was particularly Dutch. But I couldn't help but be fascinated that the exact behavior considered welcomed in one class was chastised in another.

Children in the Dutch class were learning to follow their curiosity, while children in the Scottish one were learning to control their impulses. Both seemed like useful skills, neither seemed better or worse or right or wrong, but they were so different. I wondered how classes like this reflected and shaped culture.

We'd attend several more music classes and playgroups throughout the year. In Madrid, a music class with a week-by-week curriculum, and in Valencia a class in a music school where each song introduced various instruments in the orchestra. Ella was so distraught when she had to give up one instrument and move to the next that, on three separate occasions, I had to carry her screaming to the alley behind the school wearing only our socks to give her a chance to calm down without distracting the other children.

In London I took Ella to "soft play" (which threw me off because it sounded vaguely pornographic, but of course it was not). It was a free-for-all in a giant gym, foam blocks and oversized inflated balls everywhere. There was a line out the door of parents desperate to get one of the limited first come, first served spots. Inside it was shoe-less chaos, with each caretaker simply attempting to keep eyes on their child, and a monitor at each exit to catch kids by the collar to prevent escapes.

In all our travels, the only places I was unable to find any of these pay-as-you-go mommy-and-me options was Marrakech. This was probably in part due to the fact that English is neither the first nor second language in Morocco and I was unequipped to search for classes in either Arabic or French. But, after spending two months there, it also struck me as a culture where the infrastructure for caring for children was primarily the family. There were no playgrounds, kid's menus, highchairs, or stroller-friendly sidewalks. However, of all the places we went, no one, not even the Italians, loved babies as much as the Moroccans.

BRING YOUR BABY TO MOROCCO

The medina in Marrakech was just as crowded and chaotic as forecasted. Motorbikes whizzed by inches from us in both directions ("walk left, walk right—just don't walk middle" the man who guided us to our *riad* had said). The density of the shops, the riot of colors—fabric, glassware, jewelry, rugs— was overwhelming. There were no street names, so every outing was a memory exercise, every turn had to be memorized and recognized based on what shop was on the corner.

There were no playgrounds at all in the city as far as we were able to divine. The play areas that there were occupied the top level of mall food courts and involved blinking lights and shooter games. In the two months we were in Morocco we saw exactly two highchairs, both at upscale restaurants catering to tourists.

Yet for all the lack of baby-friendly infrastructure in the country, Morocco was the most baby-loving culture I had ever come across. Walking through the medina with Ella on my chest was like being in the presence of a long-awaited, much-loved celebrity.

We would walk down the street to the sound of snaps and *coucou!*—shopkeepers snapping, cooing, and smiling to get Ella's attention. Security guards in museums waggled their fingers to make her smile. Waiters kissed her hands and picked her up eagerly if she toddled over to say hello.

One afternoon I was standing at the entrance to a shop with Ella in the baby carrier, perusing the wares, when I felt a tug. I looked down and a small, waist-high girl walking down the street with her friends had stopped to hug Ella briefly before heading on her way. As with many of these experiences, the interaction was neither with, nor meant for, me. The girl was only interested in Ella.

***

I was not expecting this. Our social circle and the internet more broadly did not seem to herald Morocco as a baby-friendly destination. We had heard before we left that Italy was a wonderful place to visit with a baby. And they did love children there. But it paled in comparison to our experience in Marrakech, where serious faces cracked into smiles whenever Ella went by.

In Marrakech, the *souks* were dominated by men. Almost all the shopkeepers and those selling their wares were men. Most of the waiters were men. This made the regular outpouring of affection even more striking, especially coming from American culture where children—and expressions of affection towards them—were still much more closely associated with women.

And this made all the difference. The medina was crowded, the sights, sounds, and smells (often unfiltered exhaust from motorbikes) could feel overwhelming on even a short stroll. Ducking into a shop was an invitation not to quietly browse but to engage, and often to negotiate, which could be exhausting.

Before we arrived in Marrakech, I had imagined that the whole experience of the medina would be all the more stressful with a child in tow. And it's true that when Mike and I left Ella with a babysitter and went out without her we could sit calmly in a restaurant or wander more slowly through a *souk*. We could get closer to fragile items without worrying about her errant kicks or grabs, and we could bargain more thoughtfully without the threat of a meltdown on the horizon.

But on the other hand, no one was blowing kisses at us. Every time we walked through the *souks* without Ella along for the trip, I missed the warmth and kind attention, the way she served as a natural point of connection and a conversation starter. Without Ella it felt like we were just two more tourists with nothing to set us apart, targets for commerce not connection, and it always felt like something was missing.

RUG SHOPPING
IN MARRAKECH

—

My favorite place from all our 303 days traveling was a rug shop down an alley near the edge of the medina in Marrakech.

The day we arrived in Marrakech from London, I was disoriented. I had awoken the morning of our flight with a high fever. I briefly wondered whether staying in a more familiar country with an excellent medical system made any sense, before shrugging off the thought. In a choice that felt ordinary at the time, and in a post-pandemic world would later be unfathomable, I popped a handful of acetaminophen and we headed to the airport, fever and all.

The truth is, being sick on a travel day was particularly unpleasant, but we got sick all the time while we traveled. After all, we were encountering endless new-to-us local variants of the cold and flu, and as such this would be neither the first nor last time illness coincided with a travel day.

And so it was that on the day of our biggest culture shock—moving from London, after four months in Europe, to Marrakech to begin two months in Morocco—I was disoriented from my fever. I could barely see straight while trying to process all that was entailed in entering a new country, in this case on a new continent where we didn't speak the language, with a culture different from any we'd been immersed in to date.

When we finally got ourselves and our luggage out of our pre-arranged taxi at the edge of the medina to walk the last one hundred yards to the private *riad*-style home we'd rented for the month, I was ready to take another round of acetaminophen and collapse into bed. Which is why it barely registered when the man who was showing us to our new home gestured to another man sitting outside a rug shop as we passed by.

"*Salaam alaikum,*" he said, hailing him, and then turned back to us. "That is Jalil. If you need anything, he is there."

We greeted Jalil as we passed, but I didn't pay much attention. It seemed farfetched that we would need something and end up rushing to a rug shop to find it.

Most days, off on one adventure or another, we'd pass Jalil on our way. He was often sitting outside his shop, sipping tea and watching the world go by. Finally, one day about a week into our stay, we decided to stop inside.

***

Jalil was warm and kind immediately, offering us mint tea and introducing us to his brothers, who were equally warm, though they spoke much less English. We accepted the tea and chatted about our trip and what brought us to Marrakech. He was shocked to find out we were spending two months in the city.

"Most American tourists, they come for a few days before they go to the desert," he explained. "The Europeans come for a long weekend."

After finishing our tea, we wandered the shop, looking at the various items Jalil and his brothers had collected from around the country: rugs, yes, but also tables and chairs, bags and jewelry, various tabletop decorations. Beautiful items that one could never lug around in a suitcase for six months.

Mike started asking questions about the various rugs, the styles and quality, the regions and tribes of origin, and Jalil lit up. He realized that in Mike he had found not just a potential customer, but an eager student.

For the rest of our two months in Marrakech, we'd return to Jalil's shop once or twice a week. We'd drink tea and discuss carpets. The shop was a *riad*, meaning it was oriented around an open, central courtyard—or in this case what used to be a courtyard but had been covered with a roof. Jalil would sit with us in the converted courtyard explaining the techniques and traditions of Moroccan carpet tying while his brothers would pull rugs from the stacks on the second story and heave them over the railing.

We'd take Ella's shoes off. I'd hold her back while the rug tumbled down, and then I'd release her to run and climb joyfully over the rolled-up carpet. Mike and Jalil would join her to unfurl it, and begin discussing the rug's history and technical details. After a few minutes the process would repeat.

In this way, Jalil's shop became the closest thing we had to a playground in Marrakech. It provided a soft, colorful place for Ella to run and crawl. But it was more than that. We came to call Jalil a friend, and were sad to say goodbye at the end of our time in Marrakech.

We selected souvenirs from Jalil's shop in the form of a half dozen rugs of various sizes, styles, and textures. We had nowhere to put any rugs, seeing as we did not have an apartment or really any clue what a future home in New

York City might look like. But when Jalil said he could ship at cost, and it became clear that buying and shipping a quality Moroccan carpet from him was cheaper than buying most of the rugs at the American chain stores, we couldn't resist.

When we finally got settled six months later in our Brooklyn rental, we'd roll out a Moroccan rug in every room, and the place would immediately feel like home.

GHOST TOWNS IN SPAIN

After two months in Morocco, we returned to Europe, flying into Madrid in early April in the rain. We spent a week there, going to museums and reveling in the things we'd missed in Marrakech, like to-go coffee and public transit. We then went on to Valencia where we spent a month drinking *vermut*, going to flamenco shows, and biking to the beach.

In mid-May, after several weeks in the urban centers in Spain, we wanted a change of pace. So, we decided to rent a car and go to the rural, mountainous north of the country, to explore the towns that dotted the feet of the Spanish Pyrenees and to take some hikes. These towns were so tiny that there was virtually no information about them online—at least not on any English language sites we could find. We contented ourselves with choosing stops based largely on driving distances on a map.

We spent ten days going from tiny town to rural hike to tiny town, staying in three- and four-room bed and breakfasts. We'd ask the proprietors to recommend hikes, and anything else there was to do in town. This led us to some odd experiences, like a tiny museum that housed a multi-level display of local taxidermied birds, and a rural recreation of the set of a hit Spanish sitcom; strange, but memorable.

We learned from our struggles with Ella in Skye back in January, our last outdoorsy destination, where she had screamed her way through more than one hike after being confined too long in the baby carrier. These tantrums had turned what would otherwise have been a delightful afternoon into an ear-splitting nightmare.

We had hypothesized that hikes with the carrier we had would be worse now than they were then. After all, that was when Ella was just shy of a year. Now she was sixteen months, and she was getting bigger, more toddler than infant. She liked to see what was going on around her, and she liked to move.

So before we left Valencia for the countryside, we went to a sporting goods store and bought a *mochila portabebé*, a framed backpack baby carrier, that we'd carry with us in our rental car for the next two weeks in the hopes of being able to do two- to three-hour hikes most days.

To tell the truth, I was a bit nervous about this stretch of the trip. We had planned a road trip through Aragón, along the Pyrenees, then down through Priorat wine country, ending up at the beach. It was the kind of plan that you would say to someone without a toddler and they'd be like, "Wow! Sounds amazing!" But to spend hours in a car, bouncing between small towns with limited infrastructure… it didn't seem impossible that we were doomed to projectile vomiting on windy mountain roads, tantrums on highways with no place to pull over, and running out of diapers with no place to restock.

As it turned out, we had our share of projectile vomiting and tantrums, but neither diminished how special this stretch of the trip was.

***

Part of it for me was that Mike had taken the lead on planning this segment, choosing the stops, picking the hikes, and suggesting the little bed and breakfasts and *agriturismos* at which we'd sleep.

Mike is not a planner by nature, while I am. While we'd co-planned most of our trip overall, I was generally the one who was a step ahead—aware of what we needed to do and parceling the work out between us. This would be the first stretch of the trip where Mike had truly and completely taken the lead. It came at a moment where I'd just met a major deadline for work, and I needed the chance to turn off the planning part of my brain for a bit. I was excited and grateful.

We spent our first night in the village of Albarricín which was tiny and charming. We did an easy hike to see cave drawings the following morning, tromping through leaves on flat ground and scampering up small hills to see 20,000-year-old cave paintings under rocky overhangs. We chatted with French tourists who'd driven over the Pyrenees for the week and were shocked to see Americans in this rural part of Spain (this would become a theme). And then we drove during Ella's nap to a working sheep farm where we stayed two nights. We met the sheep, and then the farmer served us the best lamb meal of our lives.

Our host recommended a forty-five-minute drive to a *bioparc* set on the side of a mountain. It was part hike, part zoo. We went through the turnstiles and found ourselves virtually alone in the sprawling park. The walking loop was two hours, and along the way we passed through various habitats with animals roaming sometimes alongside us and sometimes behind a chain link fence. The buffalo crossed your path, the bears and lynx you peered at from a platform. A shack halfway through the hike sold hot *croquetas*. The mountains in the background were stunning.

From there we went to Torla at the edge of a national park and did a beautiful hike to see three waterfalls. Ella fell asleep in the backpack on the way back to the start, so we decided to stop at the snack shack at the head of the trail and order some lunch. I gingerly took off the *portabebé* and stood it up next to us by our picnic bench, careful not to wake her. We ordered a hearty meal of coffees and beer, *huevos rotos*, and sausage sandwiches. That moment post-hike, feeling physically spent in the crisp mountain air, with espressos and chorizo in front of us and the baby peacefully asleep, was one of the best moments on the trip.

***

After our last major hike, we came down out of the mountains to spend two nights in a tiny town called Buera. We checked into a little inn run by a former soccer player. As we were walking through the narrow stone streets the afternoon we arrived, an old man painting his second-floor balcony called down to us to ask where we were from.

"*Hola! Hola, chicos! De dónde son?*"

I looked up. "*Hola, señor!*"

When I said we were from the United States he cursed with surprise. "*Joder!*"

"I knew you weren't from around here," he continued in Spanish, "but holy shit, the United States? How did you end up here?" He gestured at Ella, who was looking up at him with interest. "There are almost no children here, so I had to talk to you. You don't hear voices shouting like hers in these parts anymore."

He said that years ago there had been a few hundred people in this little village, but now there were seventy-six. There were just eight children.

"They will probably grow up and move to the cities to find work, just like the children before them." He gestured widely to indicate the boundaries of the tiny town. "Most of the old stone homes you are walking past are empty."

He sighed. "I have been living here for over fifty years, I remember what it used to be like. It's nice to hear a child in the streets again." He paused for a moment.

"I still don't know what you're doing here," he concluded, and then picked up his paintbrush and waved us off, conversation over.

Eight children. I grew up in Manhattan. There were probably eight children on my floor in my apartment building. I couldn't imagine what it would be like to live in the same tiny town for fifty years and to watch every year as it got tinier and tinier.

On a typical vacation, Buera never would have made it onto a list of target destinations. I was reminded again of the magic of long-term travel. We had the luxury of time to get off the beaten path and to take more risks in selecting destinations. We didn't need to prioritize the surefire destinations that friends and travel magazines swore by. We could choose a tiny town that was only a speck on the map. If it was forgettable, that was okay, because there were plenty of other destinations to come. But if a curious old man hailing us from a balcony made it one of the most memorable stops of the trip, all the better.

MAY ELLA ONE DAY
CLIMB A HUMAN TOWER

———

Whereas our road trip through rural Spain was a highlight I didn't expect, when we finished the road trip at the coast, I got the chance to check off a bucket list item that lived up to its reputation.

Decades ago, in Spanish class in high school, I'd learned about the *castilleros* of Spain. This sport involved groups of people stacking themselves into elaborate vertical castle-like structures, with the largest people on the bottom and the smallest—often kids as young as five—at the top. I'd always wanted to see the *castilleros* but had never managed to arrange my schedule to make it to Spain for the big fall festival in Tarragona.

I was scrolling on social media one afternoon in May as we were planning our last bit of time in Spain when I saw that my friend Amy had posted a video of *castilleros* from a trip she'd taken to Tarragona just a few days earlier. The big *castilleros* festival was in September... how was this possible? I messaged her.

Call the tourism office! she replied. *There aren't any competitions right now, but you can see a practice! The nearby teams come to Tarragona to practice in the piazzas around town on the weekends.*

I was thrilled. We got the practice schedule and arranged our road trip to end in a beach town not far from Tarragona so we could drive in to watch the *castilleros*.

***

As the hour for the practice approached, the plaza began to fill with locals of all ages wearing their team's colors, grabbing beers and coffees from the cafes lining the plaza. The people who were to form the base of the human castle, the largest men in the town, and the men and women that formed the next layers above, began helping each other wrap their torsos in a long white cloth, which would serve the dual purpose of providing some back support and a toe hold for the people who would climb them.

The excitement was palpable. People were shouting and toasting one another. Despite it just being a practice, there were two tables set up where the teams were selling merchandise. What had an hour earlier been a sleepy plaza outside a church was now buzzing with the anticipation of competition.

When it was time to begin, a group of musicians trumpeted the traditional tune that signified the start of the competition, and the men began to arrange themselves in a circle, clasping one another and leaning their weight into each other to build a strong foundation. The next round of people climbed up their backs, and then another round shimmied up the two layers and formed a third.

Next were the children. Slight teenagers climbed confidently up to form a fourth layer of people, standing on their elders' shoulders. And then three elementary-aged kids monkeyed their way up to form the fifth layer of the tower. As the smallest child reached the top of the human tower, now comprising two dozen people and reaching three stories tall, she hooked her legs over the shoulders of a teenage boy, tucked her heels into his armpits, and shot her hand up in the air for a momentary flourish that signified the tower was complete.

Then she wrapped her hands around the boy's neck, unlatched her legs, and slid down the backs of her supporters, followed by the other two smallest children, then the teenagers, and so forth.

It was an incredible sight. After the initial blare of the trumpets, the crowd had been completely silent until the tower was complete. When the little girl shot her hand up, there was an eruption of cheers and applause—but no one turned away or relaxed until every person had safely climbed down. Then there were hugs and high-fives all around.

I had never seen a sport so intergenerational or so communal. It was as much art as it was sport, and as much collaboration as it was competition—even across teams, as the biggest men in purple shirts leaned their weight into the teal team's base to buoy them.

A few minutes later I spotted in the crowd the tiny girl whose job was to climb thirty feet up the human tower and then to shoot her hand up in the air to claim victory. She was riding by on her father's shoulders, grinning ear to ear as she accepted the congratulations of her community.

Ella was riding on my shoulders at that moment too, so she could see over the crowd and watch this girl climb. I knew I probably should have been declaring that I'd never want her to do something dangerous like that, but that wasn't how I felt. I was thrilled by what I'd just seen. And I just hoped for Ella that she'd one day have that feeling of community, of being surrounded by people she knew, who were proud of her and were telling her so.

THE REFRAME

To finish our time in Spain we decided to spend a few days in Barcelona. Two of my business school classmates who'd married were living there at the time. We were barely acquaintances from school, but as soon as we decided to go to Barcelona, I reached out to one of them, Erin. I wanted to get her thoughts on what neighborhood to rent in, what restaurants to go to, and to see which of the must-see attractions to prioritize in our limited time in the city.

I also wondered whether she and her husband might want to meet for a drink one night. I asked as much via email a few days before our arrival.

Why don't you come over? she wrote in return. *Bring Ella.*

We took the bus from our apartment to Erin and Sebastian's, where Erin put out a spread of wines and cheeses that we carried up to the rooftop. Erin was American and Sebastian was Belgian, so I was curious how they'd ended up in Barcelona. Erin told me the story.

They were living in Silicon Valley after business school, each in jobs they loved, when Erin got breast cancer. Her tech company employer had amazing benefits and was generous with her medical leave. She recovered. But when she went back to work, she couldn't get motivated again. She had been so passionate about what she was doing before her illness, but now it seemed meaningless.

She quit. They decided to make a big change, but what? Then Sebastian got a dream job in Barcelona, and Erin was game for the adventure. Once they got to Barcelona, she decided she'd pursue her own dream: opening a wine bar. She was in the final phases of doing that now, and the bar was slated to open down the street in a few weeks.

I remember feeling stunned at Erin's story. I used to do a thought experiment when I was at my company to try to unpack for myself how I was feeling about my role. It started with a conversation with friends on our deck one sunny afternoon when we were complaining about our jobs.

"Okay," my friend asked, "If you just got told you won the lottery, would you quit your job?"

I thought about it for a moment. "No. Not right away at least. There's more I want to do with my company first, and I would want to take the time to set up a thoughtful transition before I left."

I was quiet for a moment, thinking. "But if I just got told I had only a few months to live, I'd quit tomorrow."

At the time I felt this was illuminating: I was doing something I really cared about, so I wasn't working primarily for the money. I was proud of that. Sure, I was not happy. But that could be figured out in time. So as long as I had time, I was good.

Now here was Erin saying that she'd lived a version of my thought experiment. She had been happy in her work before her diagnosis, but after being confronted with her own mortality it had upended her priorities and pushed her to pursue her dream.

I remember listening to Erin with a sudden sick feeling in my gut. In my own calculus in my thought experiment, my unhappiness at work on its own wasn't enough to warrant a change, even if I had had the total financial freedom and agency to engineer one. I needed to be confronted with my mortality, to be told that my unhappiness would persist through the last days of my life, in order to give myself permission to quit my job.

Analyzed this way, I felt less proud.

I again thought back to that weekend retreat, to the eight women who had seen me in my mental anguish and illuminated the way out. I'd neither won the lottery nor been diagnosed with a terminal illness. I was not living out my thought experiment. Yet here I was on a rooftop in Barcelona, with my family, sipping wine, feeling untethered and free. I was neither dying nor rich, but with some coaching and encouragement, I'd nonetheless managed to make the changes in my life I needed to make. I'd failed my own thought experiment, but somehow managed to make the right choice in real life.

Perhaps it was time to feel proud after all.

IF YOU FIND
YOURSELVES IN FRANCE

———

Before we left San Francisco, I posted on social media that my family and I would be taking an extended trip abroad, and I urged people to follow along on my blog if they were curious for updates. Over the next few hours I got the standard well wishes and *omg*'s of excitement, when a particular comment caught my eye. It was a family friend for whom I'd interned nearly fifteen years earlier.

We've got a house in southern France! If you find yourself that way, let me know, you're welcome to use it!

I highlighted the post and pinged it to Mike. *If we find ourselves that way?!* I thought. *This lady clearly doesn't know how we plan our travels—we will make sure to find ourselves that way!*

We picked a week in early June when the wisteria was blooming all across the facade of the ancient stone house, which sat in a tiny village outside of the tiny town of Mirepoix in southwestern France.

The village was so small that there were no addresses. The directions we were given simply listed the GPS coordinates of the village and included a photo of the house, with a warning that we'd lose cell service a few miles before we arrived.

The local caretaker, Natalie, was waiting for us when we pulled up. She was in her fifties, barefoot, and smelled of cigarettes. As often happened when we arrived in a new place, we had been warned that this house was not in the least bit childproofed. Since we'd never lived anywhere childproofed, we were used to vigilance, and this didn't bother us. However, this house had a rather extreme hazard. The knives were all stored stuck through the gaps in the slats in the ancient wooden kitchen island. For an adult, this was rather convenient—pull one out, and chop. For a toddler, this meant a dozen blades at eye level.

"I will move the knives," Natalie said as she showed us around the kitchen. She then instructed us to meet her the following morning at the weekly farmer's market in Mirepoix so she could show us where to buy the best bread, cheeses, and produce. She would have her own table set up, she said, where she'd be selling *canelé* and brioche.

***

The next morning, we drove into town. Natalie did not own a cell phone, so we figured we'd walk around the market until we found her, which we eventually did. But not at her table.

"I overslept," she said with a shrug in her thick French accent when we spotted her. "I stayed up until three making the brioche, then I slept too late to sell them." She seemed completely unbothered by this. "I'll bring them over to you later."

We wove our way through the market as she pointed out where to get eggs ("That one, not that one"), bread ("Don't buy at the market, go to the bakery down that road"), and meat ("Buy whatever the butcher in that cart offers you")—and then she went home to take a nap. We spent the next hour trying to follow her instructions. None of the vendors at the market spoke any English, but with gestures and a bit of faith we filled our baskets.

When Natalie came by later with a basket of brioche, we broached the topic of her babysitting Ella a bit while we were there. Our family friend had assured us that she had babysat all her children while they were young and would be an excellent caretaker.

"I don't know much about babies," Natalie said. "But if you think the baby will like it, sure."

Mike and I made plans to go for a hike the following day while Natalie watched Ella for a bit. We'd be back in time to put her down for her nap.

***

The next morning was a beautiful one. Natalie came over with a basket of cookies, and immediately won Ella over with dessert at 9:00 a.m. "They are all butter! Very little sugar, good for children," Natalie insisted. We shrugged and waved goodbye, figuring we wouldn't have to deal with the sugar high anyway.

We navigated our way through the winding country roads, overgrown fields giving way to the French Pyrenees as we neared our destination. We wouldn't have the chance to go as deep into the mountain range in France as we had in Spain, but we were determined to hike on the outskirts. There was an old abandoned monastery at the top of a hill, and we chose that as our destination, trudging up endless steps, rewarded with a beautiful sweeping view of the landscape.

Being with Mike but without Ella for a few hours during the day always felt particularly liberating. Like we were getting away with something. *Can you believe this? It's like we don't even have a baby!* Breathing the country air and not having to pause to check on the wellbeing of an infant was intoxicating. In these moments I felt like myself, and they made me realize how uncentered I often was when I was with Ella.

I remembered a playdate a dear friend from college and I had put together while Ella, Mike and I were visiting New York. Ostensibly it was for our daughters who were around the same age, but of course it was also for us to catch up. Yet we barely got to talk, one or the other of us being distracted nearly every moment trying to anticipate and respond to our child's needs. We'd had better conversations over text message.

I wasn't sure how to be a more centered and present version of myself when Ella was around. Until I figured that out, I needed these breaks, these hours during daylight in the fresh air with no one to take care of. They tightened my grip on the thread of my sanity.

After the hike we stopped at a small town for an early lunch, and then headed back to the house. We poked our heads inside and there was no sign of Natalie.

We went out back and there she was, dozing in the shade in a lawn chair, with a pants-less, diaper-less Ella asleep in her lap. It was too early for nap time, but then I remembered all the cookies from the morning. She had probably crashed hard.

They stirred as we approached. "She didn't want to sleep in her room, so we sleep outside," Natalie explained. "And it is good for children to be naked."

"Okay!" we said, asking no questions. "See you again, same time tomorrow?"

EVERYONE HAS
BAD DAYS

———

After being joined by friends in the villa in France, we made our way to the coast for a few days in Biarritz. From there we flew to Ireland to spend time with my parents and then to meet up with a friend from high school and her family. And from there we were scheduled to move on to Scandinavia to join another set of friends from San Francisco who were going on their babymoon.

When it was time to head from Dublin to Bergen, in Norway, I was a bit apprehensive. We had just spent about three weeks traveling with others, and were heading into another stretch of rapid travel, with four destinations lined up in ten days. But I was also excited. We were going to do another one of my bucket-list experiences: the Norwegian fjords.

We'd been through about thirty major travel days already on the trip, so it was all a bit routine. But then our flight from Dublin to Oslo was delayed, causing us to miss our connection on to Bergen.

We went to customer support and a helpful man put us on a flight that left in six hours. He said our bags didn't make our connection either, so they'd travel with us. He gave us meal vouchers. It all seemed like it was going to be fine.

We used the meal vouchers to get a very overpriced yogurt and berry smoothie for Ella, and then I put her in the carrier to try to get her to sleep. After a minute of bouncing, Ella coughed. She wailed a little. Something in her tone struck me as odd, and I only had a moment to look down at her before she reared her head back as far as it would go in the carrier and vomited. She vomited hot pink yogurt and berry smoothie all over her, all over me, and all over the floor.

We used to travel with spare clothes plus tons of wipes when Ella was really little and blow outs and spit ups were common occurrences. But at seventeen months she didn't spit up anymore and her diaper didn't leak. There was the occasional spill of course, but generally it was nothing a napkin or a wipe couldn't fix until we got to our destination.

Not so with this.

We were both soaked. We found a bathroom and approached the paper towel dispenser gratefully. But no. It was one of those endless towel types, mounted high on the wall. Wiping vomit onto the towel and then cycling it back through the dispenser did not seem effective, hygienic, or kind. Our only option was to wad up toilet paper and do our best to wipe the pink puke off me and Ella as the tiny squares disintegrated.

We had a sweatshirt for the plane in Ella's bag, so we stripped her down, and put her in it. I took off my t-shirt and contemplated it. It was completely soaked through with vomit, and was a bit ratty anyway. I threw it out.

I put on my own plane sweatshirt. Ella was sad, and uncomfortable, but seemed more tired than anything else. We left the bathroom and went back out. I put Ella back in the carrier to try to get her to go to sleep for real this time. I walked and bounced and shushed. Fifteen minutes passed. She coughed. She wailed. She vomited the other half of the smoothie.

This was all very demoralizing.

We went back to the bathroom. I took off my sweatshirt, now equally soaked with vomit. That morning I had discovered it was stained and was planning to get rid of it when we got to Bergen anyway. After eyeing the ineffective paper towel dispenser and considering the toilet paper squares, I threw it out. Ella's sweatshirt needed a wash but was not ruined. However, she had thrown up again on her pants. We took everything off. Shirtless me held shirtless, pants-less Ella while Mike went to try to buy us new clothes.

Luckily there was a small kid's section in the one clothing shop in the domestic terminal. Mike came back with an overpriced white t-shirt for me and a dress and pants for Ella. Meanwhile Ella had fallen asleep. We waited a few minutes before we couldn't stand being in the bathroom any longer. We dressed her and I put her back in the carrier. We left the bathroom.

Thirty minutes passed. She coughed. She wailed. She threw up. This time there was only berry yogurt residue. But it was enough to stain the overpriced white t-shirt. Back to the bathroom. I took off my shirt. I did not throw it out. Upon further reflection, it seemed like it might come in handy. Mike washed it, wrung it out, and put it in his bag. I put on his sweatshirt, our last adult layer that was not in our checked bags. We cleaned Ella off as best we could, out of clean clothes for her entirely and unwilling to spend another $100 on Norwegian airport fashion, and went back out.

Ella vomited twice more on the plane, including once on Mike, though mainly just saliva at that point. We landed around 8:30 p.m., a bit shell-shocked after twelve hours of travel and six vomits, and went to baggage claim. I couldn't wait to put on a clean shirt and change Ella out of her wet, smelly clothes.

We waited. And waited. The conveyer belt stopped. None of our four bags came off the belt. No car seat, no crib, no clothes. We trudged over to customer service. By the time we finished filing a lost luggage claim it was 9:15 p.m. Check-in at our overpriced hostel (which at least was affordable compared to the overpriced hotel options) closed at 10:00 p.m. The train downtown took forty-five minutes. I didn't think we could afford to miss check-in, financially or emotionally.

The information desk at the airport informed us that a cab would be only twenty minutes, and they could arrange one with a car seat. The Norwegian Air guy seemed to think this would be reimbursed. At that point though it honestly didn't matter.

When we got out of the cab, Ella threw up one final time, perched on the curb, vomiting onto cobblestones while I held her hair back. I wondered if a friend would one day do this for her in college.

We stumbled into the hostel where a perky young lady with an American accent greeted us with great sympathy, rented us towels and showed us to our room, where we had to make our own bed from a pile of sheets stacked in the corner. She could not find their baby cot.

So began a one-night experiment in co-sleeping during which Ella slept horizontally, acrobatically kicking first me and then Mike in the chest in her sound-asleep tumbling routines. We lay awake. At 1:30 a.m. the Norwegian Air lost luggage desk closed for the night. Our bags had not arrived on the last flight in. The sun rose at 4:29 a.m. We did not sleep very well.

The morning brought better news. Ella did not throw up on us overnight, or even on the extra towel we had rented to place under her. We were sleepy, and our clothes were still wet, but we realized if we microwaved them for two minutes at a time a bunch of the water would turn to steam, and we could sort of shake them out, then repeat the process. My shirt was only damp when we ventured out in the chilly morning air to the nearby H&M that miraculously opened at 9:00 a.m.

With new clothes in hand for me and Ella, and Mike wearing his sweatshirt again, plus a cup of coffee, we saw an update on our luggage tracking. It would be in Bergen by 11:00 a.m. Ella was feeling better. Things were looking up.

Around 3:00 p.m. our friends Stephanie and Rob showed up at the hostel and made their own bed two doors down. Around 4:00 p.m. our luggage was delivered. By 5:00 p.m. I was showered and in a completely clean outfit. Our ordeal was in the past, and we'd survived it. Or so we thought.

***

We spent a lovely twenty-four hours sightseeing in Bergen, grabbed an early evening cocktail, and picked up pizzas to take back to the hostel. Just as we were walking back to the hostel the world got a bit blurry; I did not feel right. Forty-five minutes later I was vomiting my equivalent of berry yogurt smoothie. I threw up six more times that evening. All the while I was thinking: I'm doomed. Not because lying on the bathroom floor of a hostel was so bad, though it was. But because the next morning we were embarking on day one of our two-day cross-country excursion through the fjords. And day one involved an early wake up, a train, a bus, and a boat.

I get *very* motion sick, always have, and always will, though it was worse when I was a child. This train-bus-boat trifecta was like a ridiculous ascent along the peak of nausea-inducing modes of transit. Train? Not bad. Bus? Depends on the roads. Boat? Always bad. *How does one survive this when simply lying down is cause for full-body-contracting nausea?* I wondered. *What if one is also responsible for a child?*

Luckily, there was Mike. Mike who'd eaten five slices of pizza and half a kebab, who almost never got sick. Thank goodness. I finally stopped vomiting at 2:00 a.m. and drifted off to sleep. I was awakened at 5:00 a.m. by rustling in the bed. Mike going to the bathroom. Mike staying in the bathroom. Mike repeatedly going to the bathroom from 5:00 a.m. until our alarms went off at 7:00 a.m.

Mike did not throw up, but his inability to do so seemed to only make his situation worse. By the time we were headed to the train, I was in decent spirits, and he was a mess. Ella, who had eaten some popcorn and raspberries for dinner and not much else in the last forty-eight hours, was still not eating much, but otherwise was doing fine. Mike was not fine.

We both suffered through the train ride, heralded as one of the most stunning in the world, as we closed our eyes against the swerving and rocking views. By midway through we'd handed Ella back to our friends and retreated into our own personal misery.

When we got off the train we figured we could take a moment to breathe, but were told that all the buses to the port left immediately, no matter what time your ferry was. Several buses were already full and pulling away. We had to board. I went into the bushes and vomited profusely, expelling all the juice and water I'd ambitiously consumed before boarding the train.

We boarded the bus. By some miracle, backwards-facing, video-watching Ella with me as her bus-fearing, just-vomited chaperone had a lovely bus trip watching waterfalls out of the oversized windows. Mike lolled his head in front of me, trying not to fall off the seat as he had a bad reaction to the anti-nausea medication we'd both taken.

We got off the bus and trudged over to the waiting area for the boat. Mike went off to find someplace to lie down. I took Ella to get something to eat. I tried to get her to eat a pancake but all she would accept was her favorite food: an orange. Finally, the moment I'd been waiting for: Ella's nap. I strapped her in the carrier, rocked her to sleep, and then found a quiet chair outside where I could lean all the way back and close my eyes. *You can do this*, I told myself.

Things seemed to be looking up. Then we went to board our 1:30 p.m. boat. There weren't very many people there; just a group of fifty Russians on a guided tour, and a few families. No one was lined up. Strange. It turned out that was because the boat had been canceled. *Don't worry*, we were told. *There is another boat in a few hours.* My spirits sank.

Then we saw that the Russians were being herded onto a boat leaving in fifteen minutes. There were a few more spaces, they admitted, but not enough for everyone else who was left stranded.

I had spent the morning sipping and then vomiting juice. I had a sleeping baby strapped to my chest. My husband was lying under a bench somewhere. I was too exhausted to stand. I was being told to wait. And I was not having it. I was getting on that boat.

I don't know if my cajoling and aggressive positioning at the head of the pack did it, or if fate intervened, but we got on that boat. I popped another anti-nausea tablet. The boat ride was lovely, and we made it to our Flam lodging without incident. Mike collapsed into bed, while Ella and I ate ramen before passing out ourselves at 6:00 p.m.

We survived.

250 MEALS OUT

———

By the end of our trip, we would estimate that Ella had eaten over 250 meals out in restaurants. Sitting down in a restaurant was as natural to her as sitting down at any other table in any of the apartments we'd rented over the course of our travels.

Ella was generally as well-behaved in a restaurant during a meal as she was at any of our various homes (which is to say, moderately well-behaved once we figured out how to get her to stop throwing food). However, we developed a number of techniques to make this possible, as a meal out often took up to three times as long as a meal served at home.

First, we'd look at the menu in advance whenever possible. Either by going online, or by grabbing one while we waited to be seated. The goal was to order our food the first time the waiter came over. No ordering drinks before food. No small talk or idle conversation between the two of us, not until after the order was placed. Chatting with the waiter was fine, and encouraged, as you wanted them to be tolerant of Ella throughout the meal, but after that first interaction they should leave with our food order.

Second, as soon as the food order was placed, one of us would get up and take Ella for a walk. She had a finite tolerance for sitting at a table, and we didn't want to use that up before there was food to be eaten. If Mike and I were going to get a chance to eat—and perhaps even to eat together—we needed to save up Ella's table time for when the food arrived.

Third, we never ordered appetizers unless it was a vegetable or a dish that was intended to be Ella's entire meal. We always hid the bread or waived away the waiter as they brought it over, since whatever Ella saw first would become her whole dinner.

Fourth, we brought our own milk, or at the very least our own sippy cup. If we brought a sippy cup filled with milk no one minded, and if the sippy cup was empty, we would ask the waiter to fill it. When we ordered a glass of milk we always got charged, but when we asked for a little milk in our own sippy cup, it was almost never on the bill.

Fifth, we would bring crayons, paper, and a book. We'd use this to buy ourselves some time while waiting if there wasn't a good place to go walk around, or if we were finished with our food and waiting for the check.

Of course, there were days when we'd ignore all of our own best practices, and just get the WI-FI password. We made it three months into our trip, until Ella was eleven months old, with no screen time besides video calls with grandparents. We had intended to make it until she was a full year old, but during a particularly difficult stretch of travel, navigating planes, trains, cars, and our own fatigue, we gave up on our goal.

We downloaded several episodes of *Sesame Street* onto our tablet, and after being shocked and relieved by how well it worked on a flight, we gave ourselves permission to work this tool into our rotation for creating calmness and patience in several public situations. Ultimately, we'd use screen time as a last resort in restaurants, too. We'd try our darndest to eat a family meal, but when all else failed, and we just needed a little more time, a few more minutes of peace to finish those last bites of our dinner, we'd put on an episode of *Sesame Street*.

***

We ate out so much over the course of the year of travel that, outside of a few notable meals, the act of eating out in and of itself was not memorable.

But there are a few meals that do stick out. Our most memorable meal with Ella was in Oslo, at a trendy upscale restaurant called Bruno. We had one night with our friends Stephanie and Rob in Oslo before they went to Copenhagen and we then reunited in Stockholm, and we managed to get a table at this restaurant.

I was always nervous about bringing Ella to fancier meals, not because she behaved any differently, but because the adult expectation at a nice meal out was to get the chance to relax, and that almost never happened.

But Ella came through for us that night. Maybe she took pity on us after the horrible seventy-two hours of the fjords, or maybe she was just too exhausted from the vomiting and travel to have energy left to burn. Maybe she took pity on our friends who had spent the first stretch of their babymoon trying to avoid catching our illness. Who knows? But that night, Ella was the perfect dinner companion.

I was worried at first because the menu was quite upscale, and Norwegian food already features many flavors that are not toddler shoo-ins, especially for a toddler who cut her teeth on pasta and pizza. But I needn't have been concerned. We ordered duck wings as an appetizer. Ella took one bite of one and did not put it down. In fact, we had to order a second round of duck wings just for her. They were eleven euros for an order of two, but I didn't care. With the duck wings, she was totally focused, calm, and happy.

In fact, the duck wings seemed to transport her. Steely Dan was playing in the background and Ella raised her arms above her head and started swaying to the music. For the next twenty minutes she ate duck wings and danced to Steely Dan while the adults sipped wine and had quiet conversation around her, content.

THE DECISION TO RETURN

———

After Oslo we went to Stockholm, where we ate our fill of *fika* and meatballs. And from there, in mid-July, we began the last legs of our trip.

We had kept our end date open for most of our travels. It had been only a few weeks earlier, at the beginning of May, while we were in Valencia, that I had started to feel it: it was time for our trip to end.

It didn't need to end immediately, but I felt like the arc of our travels had peaked, and we were on the downward slope, headed towards home. It was hard to put my finger on exactly what changed for me, but I knew part of it was realizing I'd come to dread an activity I had previously loved.

***

I had always loved planning travel. So much so that when a friend would ask for trip advice, I'd be inclined to write up long summaries of recommendations. I procrastinated by planning trips. I loved going down the rabbit hole of destination research until I found exactly what I was looking for—or something I didn't even know I was looking for before I found it.

Yet one afternoon in May, as Ella napped, and Mike and I used the down time to log onto our laptops yet again to research discount flights, affordable lodging, and kid-friendly restaurants, I sighed. As we sent yet another round of messages tapping friends and acquaintances for advice, babysitters, and connections, I realized: *I don't want to do this anymore.*

I said as much to Mike. He shifted uncomfortably.

"I'm not ready to be done," he said.

"Not immediately," I clarified. "But, look—we've got plans to travel with folks for most of June and July. So I'm saying maybe we end the trip then. Three months from now. At the end of July."

Our tentative plan had been to stay abroad through mid-September, and then to fly to San Francisco, where I had a conference to attend at the end of the month. Ending in San Francisco seemed poetic, if not exactly practical.

For one, we were a bit flummoxed by how to spend the summer months. We would have to leave mainland Europe due to visa restrictions, and all the remaining destinations on our hit list would be sweltering in July and August.

For another, ending the trip wasn't as simple as it sounded. Booking flights from wherever we were to New York was the easy part.

Then we would need to find an apartment, put Ella in preschool, get jobs. I reasoned that if we waited until October to start on these things, we'd start bumping up against the holidays. Before we knew it, we'd be still trying to get settled in early 2020. That sounded stressful and exhausting to both of us.

We didn't make a decision that day, but agreed to keep discussing it. Then, a couple weeks later, we got an invitation to the wedding of one of Mike's close high school friends. It was to take place the first weekend in August.

***

When the email with the wedding invitation came through, we stared at each other and considered the implications. At first the timing seemed bad. It was slated for six weeks before my September conference, which was to mark the end of our trip. A stop home six weeks before returning home for good seemed both inconvenient and anticlimactic. Should we skip the wedding?

On the other hand, what if we were using the wrong marker to end our trip? If instead of sealing our year with the conference, what if we used the wedding as our East Coast homecoming? It would be a chance to see friends we hadn't seen in a while, and then we could use the time between the wedding and the conference to try to get settled in New York.

We'd lose the poetry of starting and ending the year in San Francisco, and the symmetry would be broken. But of course it was a false symmetry: we were not returning to San Francisco. We'd left. Landing from abroad in San Francisco wouldn't make it a homecoming. From now on, when we went there, we'd be visitors. Regardless of the timing, our trip needed to end in New York.

The decision to end the trip was surprisingly difficult. Perpetual travel wasn't a lifestyle we would want to sustain forever, even if we could afford it. But there was so much we wanted to do and to see. The unbelievable freedom of getting to say not just "What do we want to do this weekend" but "Where do we want to be this weekend? And the week after that?" was addictive. We'd be giving that up.

On this trip, everything felt possible. That sense of freedom, of choice, and of agency was the exact opposite of what I had been feeling at the end of my time as CEO of my company. And while I wasn't going to go back to the same job, the idea of going into an office five days a week, week after week—the very thing that had seemed normal for my entire working life—now seemed limiting.

We knew that one of the major challenges we'd be tackling upon our return would be how to take the best of our year of travel and integrate it into a more conventional lifestyle. But delaying our return wouldn't make that any easier.

In the end, just as the teaching gig had been the invitation that helped us choose to launch our trip, the wedding was the invitation that helped us choose to end it. We decided to go to the wedding, and then to try to get settled in New York. We'd visit San Francisco for the conference and see our California friends one year after we'd left.

But before we tackled that, we had more urgent matters to attend to. We had our end date, six weeks out. Now we had to figure out how to end our trip.

GOING ON VACATION

———

After months of continuous and open-ended travel where the time horizon of our trip helped to remove the pressure of picking the perfect destination and maximizing every day, we suddenly had an end date. If we had an end date, we reasoned, we needed to have an end destination, too. We wanted to go out on a high note.

After pitching and debating idea after idea over cocktails, at playgrounds, and while lying in bed at night, the answer finally dawned on us. And as soon as we realized it, we knew it was obviously right: we'd end our trip by going on vacation.

Because of course the end of our trip was as much a beginning as it was an end. It was the beginning of the next phase in our lives. And it would be a lot of work to start up this new phase. We knew it would take us weeks if not months to get settled.

Our early weeks and months in New York would be filled with an unending list of logistics: we'd need to find an apartment, get things out of storage, buy furniture, get new driver's licenses, change all our addresses… We'd need to find childcare, and a pediatrician. We'd need to find jobs.

As it turned out, while we returned to the US on July 31, we wouldn't end up fully settled—two jobs, childcare, and an apartment—until November 5. And even that felt like a result of being extremely proactive, laser-focused, and of making decisions at breakneck speed.

Even before we embarked up on it, we knew the stretch of time after our return would be stressful.

What better way to prepare for it than to relax? For only the second time since we started our travels, I emailed my boss at my consulting gig to say that I'd be offline for a week. We booked flights to the Canary Islands. And to complete the feeling of being on vacation, we broke from our typical best practices of staying in apartments. Instead we used credit card points to book ourselves into resort-style hotels with swimming pools, on-site restaurants, and concierge services.

And so, 288 days into our trip, we took a ten-day vacation.

***

We flew down to Tenerife and took a cab to a giant resort that took its design inspiration from ancient Egypt. We had a top-floor room with a tiny wading pool on our balcony. It was the perfect private oasis. (That is, until Ella's swim diaper leaked and we realized we were ankle deep in poop and had to have the pool drained and professionally cleaned.)

Breakfast was included, so we stuffed ourselves each morning from the giant buffet, pocketing pieces of fruit for Ella to snack on throughout the day. I got lost twice trying to find my way back to our room from the dining area when I attempted to make the trip without Mike.

For this last leg of our journey we finally let ourselves splurge. We ordered room service and cocktails from the bar. We ate poolside for lunch, and at restaurants every night for dinner.

We booked a whale-watching trip on a glass-bottomed boat during which 70 percent of the passengers became ill.

We did not live where locals lived, nor eat where they ate. We did not go to the grocery store. We felt like tourists.

After a few days we rented a car and drove to the center of the island, where we spent two nights on the slope of the volcano Mount Teide. The area was renowned for stargazing. After Ella went to sleep each night, we snuck out of our tiny hotel room and stood in the dark in the hotel parking lot, staring over a rocky expanse, pointing at the stars.

After a few more nights by the beach, we flew up to London feeling relaxed and refreshed. We'd spend a final few days with our friends there before packing up the last of our things, and flying home.

And so, 303 days since we left the United States, we boarded our flight to New York. Our adventure was over, and the resettling would begin.

SETTLING IN

———

When we landed in New York, we were energized. Our explorations were over, and it was time now to burrow into a new community. For all the excitement of being on the move, we were now equally excited to put down roots.

The wedding of Mike's friend proved to be the perfect homecoming, giving us a chance to see a number of friends we'd missed over the past year of travel; friends whom we hadn't seen much of while living in California either. Plus, we realized, we now had a deep bank of fresh stories at the ready for any cocktail party, which made the tipsy socializing of the evening novel and fun.

At the wedding, I was making small talk with a guest I didn't know. When she found out what we had just finished doing she quipped ruefully: "Must be nice!"

I didn't demur. I knew how lucky and privileged we were to be able to do a year of travel. "It was nice," I conceded.

The majority of people perhaps can't do what we did. It was expensive. We were lucky that I was able to land consulting work that covered the cost of the trip, but not everyone's professional skill set lends itself to this. We had no obligations at home that we couldn't walk away from, even if it was difficult, painful, scary, or risky to do so. That's not true for many.

But it is true for some, including many people I know. Many of the people who said to us "I wish I could do something like that!" were the precise people who, truly, could.

***

A few days after the wedding we drove back to New York. We spent two weeks walking the city, narrowing in on where we wanted to live. After having spent so much time in European cities, with open plazas and piazzas, sidewalk cafes and green spaces dotted around the neighborhood, it was difficult to imagine ourselves settling in the dense high rises of upper Manhattan, though that was nearest to many of our friends and family. We thought back to our time in Italy and Spain, and the simple pleasure of shopping at the local butcher, bakery, and cheese shop, and recoiled at the chain grocery stores that served these apartment buildings.

So, we chose the only other place in the city where we had a cluster of friends: northern Brooklyn. We spent a day seeing apartments, and at the end of it we rented one in a converted loft-style building on the edge of Bed-Stuy, with views of Manhattan from the balconies. We moved in a few days after Labor Day. Last September we were packing, this September we were unpacking. We felt some poetry and symmetry after all.

We became members of the local food co-op, the Brooklyn Botanical Garden, and the Brooklyn Children's Museum. We chatted with mixed-race couples chasing after their own ethnically ambiguous toddlers at the Crispus Attucks playground on our corner. We chatted with a family we met at the local coffee shop about which Spanish immersion play-school they were choosing for their two-year-old as we were going through the same process for ours.

We had done it. We had pulled up all our roots, and now we were putting them down again.

***

Or so it seemed. Three weeks after we moved in, the week before I started my new job, we got a note from a real estate agent. Our landlord had sold our apartment. Technically we had thirty days to move out, but he was willing to give us up to sixty.

I peered into Ella's bedroom filled with new kids' furniture, colorful, welcoming. After moving fifty-three times in the last year, with a travel crib and a few toys the only markers of her space, she finally had a room that had been created with her in mind. Now we'd move again.

Of course, from her perspective, this was just the most kid-friendly in an endless string of temporary homes. In fact, throughout the course of our year abroad, I had noted a verbal tic: we used the word "home" to describe wherever we were living at the moment.

"Okay, ten more minutes at the playground, then home for naptime!"

"As soon as we get the check, we'll go home, I promise."

For Ella, home was a thing you left easily, never to be seen again. Home was where you slept that night, but maybe not where you slept the next night. Home was a jumping off point for exploration, and a resting place for suitcases.

I liked to think this was Ella's favorite "home" yet, but the truth is she would likely be less confounded by the move than Mike and I would, as she had no expectations that this was a place we would stay. For Ella, home was wherever the three of us were, no matter how long we'd been there, or how long we'd remain.

For me and Mike, we were tired of moving.

The real estate agent handling the apartment's sale advised us that we'd get a better deal if we waited out the sixty days he was giving us, but we were impatient. We started apartment hunting immediately. As I pored over the few listings coming on the market after the end-of-summer rush was over, I spotted an oversized duplex for rent, with its own backyard. The owners of the building used to live there, but they had moved down to Philadelphia for work. The listing online had only a few pictures, but as soon as I saw it, I knew it was our apartment. Staying in fifty-three different hotels and apartments in a year gave me a good sense of how to read an online ad.

We went to the open house and, after a cursory glance around to confirm—*yup, this is awesome*—spent the rest of the time chatting with the owners, finding commonalities and slipping in comments to demonstrate what responsible tenants we would be.

Finally, as we got ready to leave, the owner gestured at her middle-school-aged son playing video games in the corner. "You know, our son was the same age as Ella when we moved here," the owner said. "Is that right?" we murmured, mentally high-fiving one another. We were in.

***

Our final move of 2019 was in early November. It was Mike's first week of work, and we couldn't bring ourselves to pack, so we hired movers to handle it all. I explained on the phone: "We haven't packed anything. You have to pack everything." Nonetheless they were incredulous when they arrived. "You know we won't wash your dishes for you, right?"

I took the day off work and, for four hours, I washed dishes and joined them in packing, mostly as they said things like: "Don't you want your passports with you, not in a box?" or "The food in the fridge… we don't pack things like eggs and milk, you know that, right?"

Every time they pointed something seemingly obvious out, I would shrug and nod.

If only you knew, buddy, I thought, *how little I can be bothered to pack and move "properly" at this point.*

Eight hours later I was signing the final receipts as the exasperated movers returned to their truck. We were in our new home. I set Ella's room up before she arrived with Mike from preschool, and she seemed pleasantly surprised to see all her furniture and toys turn up in this latest version of home. She was unperturbed by the change.

That evening, Mike and I collapsed into bed; exhausted, but hopeful.

Over the next month we slowly acquired furniture. Our dining table was delivered on December 23, just in time for us to host Christmas Eve for my parents and brother and Alison, now his fiancée.

We were healthy, and we were together. We toasted to our Christmas in Paris the year before, recounting memories, giddy with wonder at all that had happened in our lives in 2019, bubbly with the thought of closing out the decade and welcoming a new one.

It was the first time in over ten years that I was home for Christmas—but I had not traveled to be there. I simply was home. A few days later Jonathan and Alison got married at City Hall, cementing 2019 as the year of our family coming together.

WORK IT OUT

—

Of course, when we returned in August, we knew getting settled wasn't all about our physical set up; Mike and I also needed to find full-time jobs. We took different approaches here. For Mike, once we decided we were ending our trip over the summer rather than extending it into the fall, he wanted to focus on being present and enjoying it, and decided not to think about his next gig until our return.

For me, I couldn't help but think about it. The idea of not making progress on this front was keeping me from being present and enjoying our last weeks of travel. So, I started reaching out to a few key folks in my network, letting them know that we were moving to New York at the end of the summer, and asking if they were free for coffee to be a sounding board as I explored my next career move.

As it turned out, my first meeting upon our return would be the fateful one that would lead to my new job. But when the job offer came a few weeks later, I was hesitant.

It was a senior role at an organization I deeply respected, with a mission I cared about, working with a community I felt connected to. A role where I could make a meaningful impact working with colleagues I could learn from. Ten years ago, I would have said that this exact role at this exact organization was my maybe-someday dream job.

It was that last fact that worried me. Why did I want my old self's dream job? Shouldn't I have been through some big transformation by virtue of taking this year off to travel? Shouldn't I have been using this time off as a chance to engineer a major career pivot? Achieving an old career goal seemed, perversely, like a bad outcome.

The more I thought about it, the more I realized that I was feeling burned by how trapped I had felt as a founder-CEO. I remembered how fraught it felt to extricate myself from the company I'd launched. Part of what was scary about landing my dream job was the confusion of realizing an outdated dream, yes, but part of it was the fear that it might be too good a fit—that I was diving back into something for the long haul at a moment when I deeply valued my freedom.

Over the course of conversations with the CEO and COO, we worked to rescope the role to be a two-year commitment, and it began to feel more right. Then we dropped it from five days per week to four, so that I could work on other projects on the side. I said I would think about it.

As I was describing this process to someone over coffee, they said, "Ah! You're crafting your lily pad role. This is so perfect."

I'd never heard this term before, but it instantly made sense to me. Coming off our year of travel, my priorities were not what I thought they would have been. I wasn't looking for a new adventure, or a challenge that pushed me far outside my comfort zone. I had just had that. Instead I was looking for a way to get settled and rooted in a new place. But at the same time, I was wary of commitment. I was looking for a role that struck a delicate balance: it would be a soft landing for the time being as well as a jumping off point should I care to make a career leap in the future.

It was disorienting that the role I was considering was one that I'd coveted years ago. But on the other hand, it made sense. It was a modicum of familiarity during a time of massive change.

I took the job. For good measure, I picked a start date six weeks away from when I signed my offer letter, to give myself a bit more time to get settled with Mike and Ella before turning my attention back to work. I'd start on the last day of September, the week after we returned from my conference in San Francisco.

RETURN TO REAL LIFE

———

Over the last months of 2019, we'd begin to settle into our lives, each of us finding the rhythm of our new full-time roles, which days we could leave early to pick up Ella, which pizza place delivered a pizza that was still hot.

The very things that had been most normal for most of our lives were now most novel. Spending time apart. Listening to a podcast while commuting. Making plans with friends for the weekend.

For the first few weeks at my new job, I got mid-afternoon headaches from the glare from my computer screen and the florescent lights in the office. My desk was in the interior of the floorplan and I could only see out the window by craning my neck and looking past several coworkers. I hadn't spent so much time inside for more than a year.

Yet, as we got ourselves settled, we were happy. Or, perhaps more accurately, relieved. We had done the crazy thing, made the move, taken the trip, and we'd landed. We had found an apartment, jobs, childcare. Ella was seeing her grandparents, and she was thriving. Leaving San Francisco a year ago had been scary not just because of what we were leaving behind but because of a fear that we wouldn't be able to recapture some of what we'd built. But we were doing it, slowly but surely.

After Christmas that year, we drove down to Pennsylvania to meet up with a few friends from Washington, DC for New Year's Eve. We rented a house in Amish Country, in part for the novelty of it and in part simply because it was equidistant.

After a day of horse and buggy rides and feeding pygmy goats, we cooked dinner with our friends and put all the kids (six under six between the eight of us) to bed before popping champagne to sip until midnight.

It was hard not to get swept up in the notion that we were entering a new decade and that we'd lined everything up just in time. We'd worked on, moved through, moved past, and shed so much of what wasn't working for us in the past decade.

The New Year's prior we'd been with friends in Skye, Scotland, three months into our trip. Ella had just taken her first steps and said her first word. New Year's 2018, the year before, I had been eight months pregnant, preparing to meet my board members to resign as CEO.

I could rewind through every New Year's of the last decade. All the way back to New Year's 2010, which set the tone for the decade to come. Mike and I were preparing to move in together in January, and he would propose a few weeks later in March. We'd spend 2010-2018 building: our careers, our family, our lives. In 2019 we'd take an exhausted break from everything we'd built. Contemplating the last decade of choices and changes made my head hurt.

But looking ahead to 2020 I only felt optimism.

That New Year's Eve leading into 2020 we were with our old friends, sitting around, reminiscing, getting a bit drunk and a bit philosophical. "Okay," one of our friends proposed, holding up her glass. "Rate 2019 from one to ten."

It had been a hard year for most. Challenges at work, sicknesses and surgeries, deaths in the family, adjustments to and challenges with partnerships and parenting. The ratings varied, but many of them were low. 2019 had been a hard year.

Mike and I went last. "Um, I guess I'd give it a nine?" he said.

I chimed in, "I was going to say eight only because I didn't want to make anyone feel bad."

The year of travel had not been easy. In fact, in many ways it had been one of the harder things I'd undertaken. But it had been surprisingly free from angst, self-doubt, and chronic stress. There were moments—even stretches—of loneliness, boredom, frustration, exasperation, and sadness over the year.

Yet there were so many feelings I was used to feeling regularly that were not present: chronic and compounding stress, anxiety, and a relentless compulsion to compare my life to those of others around me and to find mine lacking. In 2019, I realized, for the first time in a very long time, I had largely been at peace with myself and my choices. It was a foreign feeling, and it was easy to toast.

I went back to work after the holidays refreshed, relieved by how much we'd managed to get settled in the last months of 2019, and ready to move into something that felt more like a steady state in the new year.

"New year, new decade, new you!" my coworker Camila would quip in the first weeks of 2020, a joke-y expression of empowerment whenever one of us was making a choice around the office. Whenever she said it, I would feel a giggle rising in my chest. It really felt like a new me, and I was ready for the new decade.

WORKING WITHOUT INFRASTRUCTURE PART 2

———

I was at a conference in late February 2020, chatting with a colleague about an event his company was hosting at the end of March. We were wondering whether he'd have to cancel it due to COVID-19. I remember thinking at the time that it seemed like an aggressive move, but that I could understand wanting to be conservative.

Two and a half weeks later, on March 11, I had a completely different perspective. I was packing up my bag at the end of the day at the office, when I paused. The day before, someone at World Trade Center 4, the seventy-four-story office building where Mike worked, had tested positive for COVID, and they'd evacuated the whole building. The following day at my office we were doing a work from home drill, just in case something similar were to happen to us. Meanwhile, I was becoming increasingly uncomfortable taking the subway.

I thought for a moment, then made some space beside my laptop in my handbag and threw in my keyboard and mouse. Then I pulled a fistful of snacks out of my filing cabinet drawer. I had a suspicion our work from home drill might be more than a drill. I didn't know when I'd be back in the office next and didn't want to attract mice.

Sure enough, that weekend New York City entered lockdown. On Sunday night March 15 we got an email from Ella's little Montessori school: following NY Department of Education's decision to close schools beginning the following morning, Ella's school was shutting down, too.

Working parents citywide went into a tailspin figuring out how to handle the upcoming workday, much less workweek. Mike and I were both fortunate to have flexible employers who supported our need to balance caring for Ella with all the meetings, projects, and decisions that were on our respective plates. But nonetheless we were immediately drowning.

We'd trade off time with Ella based on who had immovable meetings, or meetings where a toddler would be particularly disruptive. We'd try to give her our undivided attention for at least a few hours a day, counting on her favorite videos and naptime to buy us some more precious minutes to work. We'd open our laptops again as soon as she was down for the night.

It was awful, but it still felt temporary. Surely we'd be in lockdown for a couple of weeks—perhaps a month?—and then back to normal. Yet as the days passed, COVID numbers surged in New York. Deaths ballooned soon after. They built a field hospital in Central Park. Flour, toilet paper, and all types of disinfectant were impossible to find. Normal began to feel frighteningly elusive.

***

On March 24, we got another email from the director of Ella's school: she was closing it down—for good. Unsure whether she could weather the pandemic, she chose not to even try.

Just a few weeks earlier we'd confirmed the fact that we were enrolling Ella in preschool there again in the fall. This not only destroyed our near-term childcare plans, but also our vision for Ella's upcoming education. We were stunned.

But only momentarily. We thought back to our year of travel—all the time we'd spent negotiating our own needs with Ella's with little to no support. And that was at a time when only one of us was working part-time. We considered how haggard we were already, after only ten days of full-time working plus full-time parenting. It was not sustainable.

With her school closed for good, we didn't owe any more tuition as of April 1. It only took a moment of discussion to decide what to do. We raced to contact the lead teacher from the school, now out of work. Any chance she'd be interested in serving as a nanny?

As it happened, two other families had the same idea. So, by April 1, we'd formed what would in the coming months come to be known as a "pod."

We didn't feel comfortable sending Ella to the pod right away, not while hospitals were still at max capacity and ventilators were in short supply. Not while a case of COVID could land you in a tent in Central Park. We decided to wait until the situation in New York had stabilized and numbers were trending down. Since hospitalizations were a lagging indicator of infections, we figured that by the time they peaked and began dropping, we could consider sending Ella to her pod.

By the end of April, we considered our options. We both believed the pandemic was going to continue indefinitely, and that we needed to be planning for months, not weeks.

And we agreed that our current situation was not sustainable. Either one of us could quit our job, or we could send Ella to her pod. Another break in our careers seemed risky for either of us. We chose the pod.

By May 1 we had childcare and, amidst the global chaos, our personal and professional lives had somewhat stabilized.

As we watched friends with kids agonize over their own plans, we credited the swiftness in our decision-making to our experience traveling. I did not believe there was an objectively right or wrong choice to be made—but there certainly was a best choice for us, and probably for many families. And after so much practice in joint decision-making, we knew how to run the analysis for ourselves, quickly. Completely isolating the three of us had its advantages of course, but we knew the truth: for us, it was not sustainable.

We would weather the pandemic together, largely in isolation—but with childcare.

WHERE IS THE BACON?

——

The combination of our new priorities upon our return to the US followed by the lockdown of the early phase of the pandemic made for some weird breaks in our family habits that we had developed while traveling, including our eating habits. In particular, a year into our return the quotidian nature of eating at a restaurant would seem an absurd memory.

Right after our return, we relished the novelty of regular, reliable babysitters and reveled in the chance to eat out, just the two of us, without the choreography of creating a successful meal with a toddler. We also preferred to eat later than 6:00 p.m. So, every other week or so, we booked tables for two, or met up with friends, and left Ella at home with a sitter.

But mostly in those months after our return, we didn't eat out at all. After a year of travel, it was eating at home that was the real novelty: the chance to cook something that required more than a few ingredients. A stocked pantry with spices, flour, sugar, sauces. The opportunity to shop for what was needed for a recipe, knowing that if there were leftover ingredients they'd get used at a later date, not discarded in a week or two when we packed our suitcases.

I cooked things I'd never cooked before: chicken piccata, lamb burgers. I baked banana bread repeatedly, experimenting with different ratios of white and whole wheat flour.

Staying in, the notion of staying anywhere, was novel.

Of course, in March of 2020, six months after our return, staying home went from an opportunity to an obligation. New York City went into lockdown and eating out became a relic of the past, something to pine over.

At the start, we didn't miss eating out. We'd had our fill, and there was too much else to worry about—finding toilet paper and hand sanitizer, childcare, COVID rates spiking across the city and in our own neighborhood. Plus, we were very clear as the pandemic wore on that the ability to stay at home was a privilege.

Nonetheless, we soon began to miss the simple pleasure of someone else not just cooking our food (which we could of course replicate via delivery services) but of someone else cleaning up after us as well. The chance to end a meal with a hearty "thank you" as opposed to a pile of dirty dishes.

When restrictions lifted in New York City and outdoor dining was once again allowed, we left the house early one Saturday morning to go out to breakfast at a local diner with an outdoor patio. On the way, we discussed with Ella what was happening.

"We're going to eat at a restaurant," we explained.

"A restaurant?" she said, perplexed. It was August. Ella had just turned two and a half. I reflected for a moment and realized that she had not eaten at a restaurant for over six months. Was she even able to conjure coherent memories from before she was two? Without the ongoing experience of dining out creating a thread of continuity and familiarity with the practice, had those 250 meals eaten out while we were abroad just vanished from her consciousness?

"It's a place where you sit at a table and someone else makes your food and brings it to you," I explained. We got settled at a table, six feet from our neighboring diners, and looked at the menu.

Ella looked around. "What's *that*?" she pointed at the menu. "What are *they* doing?" she pointed at the other patrons. "Who is that *man*?" she pointed at the waiter. I remembered that, at that stage in the pandemic, she wasn't used to spending any sustained time around strangers.

"They are also eating at this restaurant. And that man will bring us our food."

She considered this. "Can I have bacon?"

I considered this. "Yes."

The waiter approached, and I ordered her a waffle with a side of bacon. He walked away.

"Where is it? Where is the bacon?"

"They are cooking it, in the kitchen."

"Can I go see?"

Most evenings at our apartment, I'd call Ella to the table when dinner was already served, her wait time down to zero. Other days, she'd sit up on the counter while I cooked, watching the progress of our meal. In the last six months, she'd completely forgotten how a restaurant worked.

It was proof of what we'd suspected. That, as much as Ella had been on the trip with us every step of the way, present and participating and influencing and impacting every choice and moment of our experience—she herself would never remember any of it. It was strange to think that a year that would be singled out in our memories forever would be a curiosity in pictures for her.

"We have to wait here, kiddo," Mike said as he pulled the pen and paper we had brought with us out from under the stroller. And he and Ella started drawing squiggles while we waited for bacon.

UNSTUCK TOGETHER

———

It was nearly six months into quarantine in New York City, in September 2020, and it was Mike's night to do bedtime with Ella. They had just gone downstairs and, after spinning in circles for a few minutes trying to decide whether to clean the kitchen or get back on my laptop to work, I decided to do neither of those things.

Our collective spirits were low. In what had at one point been the epicenter of the COVID-19 pandemic, we were largely confined to our apartment. We'd moved to New York to be close to friends and family, but it was now unsafe to see them. Days in the apartment blended together in a sort of haze.

The weather had also hovered strangely all spring. It seemed to be forty-eight degrees and drizzling for a month. We were fortunate to have found an apartment with some outdoor space. In fact, one of our realizations from our travels was that we were always happiest when we had a sliver of private outdoor space. The chance to step outside without packing up a stroller, or to be able to feel the sun on our faces while Ella slept, had a huge impact on our mental health.

But then all spring we had simply stared at our damp little brick yard with our noses pressed against the window and breath fogging the glass, waiting for the weather to turn enough for us to enjoy it.

Even with the summer's warm weather and local COVID infections under control, there were few places to go. With the three of us almost always at the house, I was finding precious few moments of repose between work, time with Ella, time wasted being generally anxious and reading the news, and sleep. Without a commute, or exercise classes, or work travel, I was back to having virtually no alone time. And when we wanted to hang out with friends, we again had to do so via video call.

In a bizarre dark poetry, the challenges of isolation during the pandemic proved to have much in common with the challenges of exploration during our year of travel. Except this time the payoff was not measured in an abundance of experiences, but in a lack of exposure. No new cultures, or sights, or cuisines. Just another day in our apartment, not getting sick.

So that evening in September, when I found myself with thirty minutes of solitude, I decided to give myself a break, and instead of a laptop or a sponge, I picked up a book.

∗∗∗

The book was Elaine Welteroth's 2019 memoir *More Than Enough*. I was a few chapters in, and Elaine was describing a conversation she'd had in her last year of college with a mentor of hers and another student. The trio took turns revealing their deepest wishes, and then reacting to each other's revelations. Elaine shared her dream to work in magazines. She described how these smart, supportive women built her up in that moment of vulnerability. She then went on to share the lessons she drew from this, including that the voices of strong, supportive women can be pivotal in one's life.

I almost fell off the couch. Elaine's description was so similar to my own experience three years earlier that in my strained, pandemic-addled state I actually had a moment where I wondered if that girls' weekend in Palo Alto was real, or just a fantasy inspired by a story I'd read in a book. I had to ground myself in the fact that the weekend had in fact taken place in Palo Alto in 2017, the life-altering advice had propelled me on a trip around the world, and now I was on the other side of the adventure, reading a book on a couch in Brooklyn in 2020.

It was a perfect reminder: I was not so unique. If a group of women could liberate me, and a group of women could liberate Elaine, perhaps the right group at the right time could liberate anyone. And if my experience wasn't so unique to me, then maybe it also wasn't so unique to that moment in time.

It was easy to feel the walls closing in again that pandemic spring and summer. But it didn't mean they couldn't be knocked back down in the future. I had escaped when I felt trapped once, and I could do it again. The book in my lap, I processed these thoughts. Before long I found myself sobbing—with relief.

***

The last few months it had felt impossible not to draw comparisons between where we were at that moment and where we had been a year earlier. The differences were stark. In fact, my phone would buzz daily with a notification from my photos app: *This was you, a year ago today!*

Ding!—me, Ella, and Mike at our favorite rug shop in Marrakech.

Ding!—me, Ella, and Mike playing soccer in a tiny plaza in rural Spain.

Ding!—me, Ella, and Mike on a sheep farm in Ireland.

And every morning, I looked up from my phone and out at a painfully identical day: me, Ella, and Mike at home during a global pandemic.

It was easy to see those photos as reminders of what was, and what had been lost. But reading that scene in that book and remembering my own pivotal conversation over that girls' weekend three years earlier had shifted my perspective. When I managed to see those notifications as reminders not of the past but of the potential for the future, I did not feel sad, or stuck. I felt grateful.

I was grateful for the past: that we did not wait to make the changes that we needed to make in our lives, that we had traveled when we could, and that it had helped us get closer as a family.

I was grateful for the present: my health, my family's health, and that we had a safe place to stay and steady employment.

I was grateful for the perspective I had gained on the future: that it is full of possibility. And that we can make big changes as needed to shape it.

From now on, I reminded myself, we might put down roots and we might make commitments, but that did not mean we were confined by our past choices or our present circumstances.

This trip had proved that to me. As sticky as it might feel in this moment and in future ones, we were not stuck. We were unstuck, together.

ACKNOWLEDGEMENTS

———

The biggest thank you goes, of course, to Mike. It's easy to take for granted that we were aligned on the need to take this trip. But I know that not everyone's spouse would also believe that a year of travel with an infant is not only doable, but a very good idea. Thank you also to "Ella," for making this trip more memorable than any past vacation, and for being adaptable and curious, and for not giving us cause to give up and come home early.

Thank you to all the people who came to visit along the way, especially to my parents and Mike's mom who came multiple times, and especially to those who brought your own babies on their first international adventure (Shireen and Mack!). Thank you to all our hosts: Alisha and Carlos (repeatedly), Bisan and Fabrizio, Ina and Jeffrey, Carla and Tony, and Mohammed. And thank you to all the friends who made connections who proved invaluable along the way.

Thanks to everyone who read parts and drafts of this book, and who provided feedback, especially Mike and Alisha and Jonathan.

Thanks to everyone who backed this project in pre-sales: Jonathan and Alison, Kathryn, Mom and Dad, Anamaria, Tristan and Amoy, Ann, Mike, Marina and Brad, Alisha and Carlos, Nick, Jennifer, Mina and Shahab, Mar and Pete, SAS and Rob, Eric, Marc, Josuel, Katie, Amber, Margaux, Robert, Joey, Carrol, Bec, Erin, Will and Linsday, Randy, Cherizza, Alex, Jeannette, Raymond, Maryam, Vanessa, Sharon, Adam, Naima, Suzy, Beatrice, Sabrina, Cassandra, Jessica, Alex, Lauren, Nigel, Christina, James, Maria, Judd and Ilana, Ross, Camila, Jill, Sumi, Eunice, Erin, Bryant, Abe, Che, Travis, Angie, Stephanie, Elizabeth, Nate, Csaba, David, Bining, Catherine, Monica, Sharyanne, Ruth, Dan and Alison, Bryce and Sandra, Christine, James, Lav, Amanda, David, Michael, Yusef, Landon, Sinohe, Emma, Paige, Omoju, Joan and Ken, Zina, Nancy, Nat, Julian, Julia and Vijay, Kyle, Mark, Elizabeth, Harlyn, Alex, Marion, Vanessa and Lin, Lindsay, Karen, Amanda, Amber, Celena, Kate, Brian, Therese, Tommy, Wes, Elizabeth, Jane, Chuck, Christina, Meredith, Jordan, Rachel, David, Negin, Tammy, Adrianna, Jim, Arthur, David, Chris. The backing was much appreciated, but the vote of confidence and the accountability was priceless.

Thanks to Eric for creating a system and structure that dragged me kicking and screaming through this process. Thanks to the NDP team for your help turning an idea into a Word doc into a reality.

And thanks to you for reading.

CPSIA information can be obtained
at www.ICGtesting.com
Printed in the USA
BVHW042324201220
596047BV00008B/22